The Stress-Free Guide To Studying In The States

A Step-By-Step Plan for International Students

Toni Summers Hargis

The Stress-Free Guide to Studying in the States:
A Step-By-Step Plan for International Students

by Toni Summers Hargis

First published Great Britain 2013 by *Summertime Publishing*

© 2013 Copyright Toni Summers Hargis

ISBN 978-1-909193-42-0

Cover and layout by Owen Jones Design
www.owenjonesdesign.com

"A very thorough introduction for international students considering university study in the US, this book covers everything from vocabulary and abbreviations through campus life and academic culture. Definitely a must-read for parents and students unfamiliar with the application process in the US."
Amanda Eckler, Assistant Director for Programs, Yale University, Office of International Students & Scholars (OISS)

"For international students trying to decide which US university to choose, and then navigate the complexities of the application system, the comprehensive advice in this guide is a must-read."
Louise Tickle, Award-winning Education and Social Affairs Journalist. http://louisetickle.co.uk. @louisetickle

"The jargon, the cultural differences and the inside track on the application process are all explained in this guide for anyone thinking about studying in the US."
Sean Coughlan, BBC News education correspondent, Education Journalist of the Year 2011, @seanjcoughlan

"Wise advice demystifies the process, from first thoughts about an application to arrival and settling in, and makes this excellent book an essential 'must-buy' guide for applicants, parents and school Higher Education applications staff."
Peter J. McDonald, Director of University Entrance, Magdalen College School, Oxford, England

"Applying to university or college in the USA is a minefield for those studying outside the country. In this Guide however Toni Hargis has succeeded in 'demystifying' what is in essence a very complex process in a thoroughly clear and comprehensive manner."
Julia Douglas, Head of University US Applications, Sevenoaks School, Kent, England.

Dedicated to my own hard-working students,
Cydney, Aidan and Cal

x

About the Author

 Toni Summers Hargis is a Brit who has lived in the USA since 1990. She is mother to three YankeeBrits, all of whom are plowing their way through the American education system. Educated at Bristol University, England, and Loyola University, Chicago, Toni has first-hand knowledge of student life on both sides of the Pond and is so far surviving her experience as a parent in the US college application process.

Toni is the author of *Rules, Britannia; An Insider's Guide to Life in the United Kingdom*, (St. Martin's Press) the popular book for Americans visiting the United Kingdom. She also blogs as Expat Mum (http://expatmum.blogspot.com) is a featured columnist for *Expat Focus* (www.expatfocus.com), and for BBC America's *Mind the Gap* (www.bbcamerica.com/mind-the-gap), and has appeared on TV and radio to discuss UK/ US matters. In her spare time Toni runs *Caring Kid Connections* (www.caringkidconnections.com), a charity she founded in 2009 to help school children in Ghana.

Visit *The Stress-Free Guide To Studying in the States* web site at www.stress-freestudyinthestates.com

Acknowledgments

Although I say throughout that this book brings together information from all over the Internet, it also contains invaluable advice from professionals in the field and from individuals who have gone through the process. My sincere thanks to the following people who generously gave me the benefit of their expertise and experiences.

High school, college Admissions, and International Office professionals who offered up their time and attention at probably their busiest time of the year – Matthew Beatty, Director of International Admissions, Indiana University; Clare Brown, Head of Careers, Caterham School, England; Julia Douglas, Head of University US Applications, Sevenoaks School, England; Amanda Ecklar, Assistant Director, Yale University OISS; Rendy Schrader, Director of International Student and Scholar Advising, Indiana University. I also picked the brains of Hamilton Gregg, International Education Consultant, China, and Mary Beth Marklein, *USA Today* Higher Education writer.

To my Beta readers and to the students and parents who took the time to talk about their own experiences, thanks for your time; I know how busy you all are – Alix Bell (UK), Cydney Hargis (USA), Stephanie Healy (UK), Joe Holleran (Brit in the USA), Rena Nathanson (American in the UK), Johara Nour (Thailand), Kamel Osman (American global citizen, currently in the USA), Tanya Rehki (Indian in the USA), Jennifer Taylor (former college Admissions professional and current high school College Counselor, Chicago), Juliana Tamayo (Columbian in the USA).

A huge thank you to my fabulous editor Jane Dean, who makes my work look exponentially better than it is, and to my publisher, Jo Parfitt, who has supported my work since the day we met in Houston, Texas, back in 2007.

And finally, although she probably didn't realize what she was saying at the time, thanks to my long time friend Mandy Kemp for those immortal words, "This should be your next book."

A Note from the Author

Applying to any college is exciting – applying to study in a foreign country can be daunting, because of the unfamiliar application process, the need to obtain a student visa and the whole idea of operating in a different culture.

There are many good books, web sites and consultants to help potential American undergraduate students submit the best application they can, craft winning personal essays, and obtain financial aid or athletic scholarships. In addition, there are consultants and numerous US government web sites giving you the rules and regulations relating to Non-Immigrant visas. The problem is, while the information is all out there on the web, it's often difficult to find or make sense of, and if you don't have the extra money to pay a consultant, you can be put off before you've started.

Help is here!

The Stress-Free Guide to Studying in the States brings all this information together for the first time, at an affordable price. As an international applicant to an American undergraduate program, *The Stress-Free Guide to Studying in the States* gives you a comprehensive, step-by-step plan for the entire process so you can decide how much you want to tackle yourself, and how much help you may need to enlist. Let me stress that negotiating the US college application process, and obtaining the necessary visa, is entirely manageable on your own and this book will help you succeed without paying big bucks to a consultant or agency. URL addresses for all relevant web sites are provided so the information you access is always up-to-date.

To begin, I would advise you to read through this book before making any decisions or taking any action. It is important to understand the big picture of the application and visa process, in order to manage your time and avoid unnecessary panic and stress.

Keep calm and remember to breathe!

Toni Summers Hargis
www.stress-freestudyinthestates.com

Table of Contents

Introduction

"It was a complete and utter nightmare."

"I hadn't a clue where to start."

"I didn't have the time to do the research."

"The information is all over the place."

These are just a few of the comments I received from non-Americans while writing this book. As a foreigner myself I found the whole process overwhelming when my daughter began her college applications, and I was very glad she knew what she was doing.

As many American high school students will tell you, the college application process can be a nightmare. Application forms are long and comprehensive, often taking days, if not weeks, to complete. US colleges take a much more holistic approach to deciding which students they make offers to, and many foreign applicants are not used to writing so much about themselves. Gone are the days when applicants simply reported their academic results and waited – now you're expected to talk about your extra-curricular activities, demonstrate leadership or otherwise convince the college Admissions department *you* will be an asset to their student body.

Deadlines are not all the same, nor do you necessarily hear from colleges at the same time. There is no central application body for colleges so students are required to keep track of multiple applications on their own. It's not surprising students from outside the USA might be overwhelmed and confused by the college application process.

Once you have successfully tackled the college application section of the nightmare, you're faced with the visa application process. This has the potential to be even more of a challenge depending on your circumstances and country of origin.

Fortunately the US government and its consular offices around the world are easier to work with now the information is available on the Internet – you can easily learn what's required and track your applications online. Before the Internet you had to sit back and wait for your envelope to be returned to you because you'd omitted one vital document. Now most of the application is completed online it's far less likely documents and forms will be lost in the process, and you have a better idea of how long everything will take.

The Institute of International Education states in its November 2012, *Open Doors* report – www.iie.org, that the number of international students in the USA in the 2011/ 12 academic year grew to a record 764,495; an increase of over 31% since 2001/ 2002, and a 5.7% increase on the previous year. Many of these students came from countries whose education system and culture is very different to that of America. The top three countries with the most students studying in the USA are China, India and South Korea.

For international students thinking about attending an undergraduate college in the USA, *The Stress-Free Guide to Studying in the States* helps meet the challenges of this new adventure. It gives practical advice, information and resources for all aspects of the college experience, imparts cultural information in an engaging yet useful way, and lessens some of the tension surrounding this huge step.

The Stress-Free Guide to Studying in the States covers not only the application process, but also the pre-application thinking process. In addition, it gives pointers for helping you find your feet when you first arrive at college, examples and nuggets of advice from real people who have survived the ordeal or are professionals in the field. Deciding you might like to attend college in the USA is an exciting thought, but the practicalities can be off-putting. With this book, good organizational skills, sufficient time and a lot of deep breathing, you will be able to manage the application process perfectly well and cope with a strange college environment to boot.

What makes this book so relevant for international students?

It's written by an expat Brit who knows what it's like to come to the States as a 'foreigner'. Not only have I studied at both a British and an American university, and currently have children in the American education system, I have personally navigated the US immigration system and survived the agony that can be the 'college app' process.

Toni Summers Hargis
www.stress-freestudyinthestates.com

The Thought Process

While there's a lot to think about when looking at colleges in the USA, it helps to think clearly and chronologically. You can't do everything at the same time and there is a definite order to your questions and action points.

Is a US college feasible?
Chapter 1 – Thinking of Studying in the USA?

Familiarize yourself with the US college system and vocabulary
Chapter 2 – An Overview of US Colleges

Narrow down your choices
Chapter 3 – What to Consider When Choosing a College

Can't afford the fees?
Chapter 4 – Funding your College Degree

How to apply
Chapter 5 – The College Application Process

ACT or SAT? Understanding the ACT and SAT tests
Chapter 6 – Standardized Tests

Hearing back from colleges
Chapter 7 – Offers and Rejections

Visa process and other important steps
*Chapter 8 – Before You Go – Visa Application
and Other Important Steps*

What to do when you get to college?
Chapter 9 – On Arrival

Finding your feet at college
Chapter 10 – US College Life – The Lowdown

Learning the American Way
*Chapter 11 – The American Language
and Customs*

What parents need to know
Chapter 12 – Notes for Parents

Chapter One
Thinking of Studying in the USA?

If you've picked up or downloaded this book, you're obviously giving some thought to attending college in the USA. Great – keep going. More and more foreign students are doing it, and American colleges are actively encouraging it, so it's not a pipe dream. Even if your high school has no experience in sending students to college in the USA, this shouldn't be a barrier to you.

Before getting too far into the details think carefully about the realities. There is a lot involved in getting to a college in the USA and it can seem perplexing and daunting at first. Here are a few points to consider (details on all points follow in subsequent chapters).

Using a consultant

Many international students hoping to attend a US college turn to consultants and experts to help them or to manage the entire process. These companies will help you narrow down the colleges to look at, assist with applications and manage the visa application process, but some would-be applicants find they cannot afford these additional fees. As I explained in the introduction, there is nothing secret about US college or visa applications, and (especially with the help of this book) most families will be able to handle the process as long as they allow sufficient time. Before making a decision about hiring a consultant, read this book to get a realistic idea of the time and effort you'll need to apply to colleges in the USA.

If you do engage a consultant, check the small print on the web site or the printed materials before signing up. While they may advertise a specific sum for their services, there can be many additional costs along the way. It is important you (or your parents) know the full financial commitment before you begin working with them. Don't be embarrassed to ask about additional costs that might arise. Running out of funds halfway through the process may mean you suddenly have to manage a process you know nothing about.

> **⚠ WARNING**
> If your consultant insists on only looking at a few colleges without encouraging you to look at others, ask whether he or she is working in collaboration with these colleges. Although some consultants will point to specific colleges because they believe they are the best fit for you, some are being paid a commission by individual colleges to attract international students. It is in your best interests to know if your consultant is being paid a commission in this way.

Hamilton Gregg – www.hamiltongregg.com, an international Education Consultant based in China, advises:

'When students are looking for someone to help they should consider the following: Does the agent have the student's best interest in mind? This is very hard to determine as one never knows or can tell.

★ *Families should run, run quickly, from anyone who 'guarantees' admission to a school or set of schools. There are no guarantees, ever.*

★ *What is the background of the consultant/ agent? Are they educators and do they know anything about the schools, your major or what the school is like?*

★ *Are they cutting corners – falsifying documents to help the student gain entry? This is tricky as foreign education systems are often not in line with US college expectations (i.e. the academic information doesn't always fit neatly into a US college application form).*

★ *Is the consultant a true professional in the field? What are their qualifications? For example, the Independent Educational Consultants Association – www.iecaonline.com* is very stringent in their acceptance of consultants, requiring an M.Ed., proven success in admissions work, letters of recommendation from families and university admission staff who know the individual, a list of schools the consultant has visited personally, and a guarantee that members will follow strict ethical guidelines such as not accepting commissions from schools, not writing essays or falsifying documents etc. Many Agents cannot ever qualify.'*

You can find reliable assistance and advice from the Education USA advising network, which is supported by the US Department of State's Bureau of Educational and Cultural Affairs (ECA). It provides advice and support to students in 170 countries around the world who are interested in studying in the USA. Visit the web site for information and to help find an advisor near you – https://www.educationusa.info/about.php.

---

* Please note – all web sites cited in this book, with particular reference to government web sites, are prone to changes in design and format which may affect their URLs

In addition, NACAC (National Association for College Admission Counseling) is closely monitoring international education consultants. For a deeper understanding of the issues, visit their website – http://www.nacacnet.org/studentinfo/InternationalStudentResources/Documents/InternationalRecruiting.pdf.

Applications

Timeline

Like most professionals in the field, Matthew Beatty, Director of International Admissions at Indiana University, stresses the importance of starting early when applying to US colleges. ThinkEducationUSA – www.thinkeducationusa.com, recommends you allow at least a year between your first college search and the date you would like to start classes at an American college:

★ The first six months should be a time to research all that will be required of you. This book will cut down on some of the research time by making the information available in one place, but exploring your options and examining your favorite colleges closely can still be a time-consuming activity. If you are looking for financial aid this will add additional time to the research stage.

★ Twelve months before your intended start date, ThinkEducationUSA recommends you register for any required standardized tests such as the ACT, the SATs or TOEFL. The results of these tests take several weeks to come back and you may not be able to apply to colleges without this information. (See *Chapter Five – The College Application Process* and *Chapter Six – Standardized Tests (ACT and SAT.)*

★ Once you have the scores from your standardized tests (above), you must allow time for those scores to be officially reported to the colleges you are applying to.

★ Your applications should begin seriously in the fall/ autumn **before** you wish to attend college (assuming you're looking to begin in the fall/ autumn). In most cases you won't receive a college offer till March-May of the following year, and you cannot begin your visa application without a firm offer and acceptance.

★ The visa application can take anything from a few weeks to several months.

★ The College Board (which administers the SAT test) has a suggested two-year to-do list to prepare for applying to American colleges – http://international.collegeboard.org/study-in-the-US/resources

There is no overarching organization through which you apply to American colleges. Many now use the Common App form (see *Chapter 5 – The College Application Process*), which saves duplication of material but does not administer individual college applications, and each individual college will request supplementary material. However you apply, many colleges have different deadlines, application requirements and academic standards – some take extra curricular activities into account while others rely solely on academic scores. Applying to college can be a minefield even for American students, and although it is extremely manageable, it will take commitment and effort.

Note for Americans living abroad

If you are a US citizen living outside the USA and plan to return to the US to attend college, you can apply as a regular undergraduate applicant. If you have not attended an American school you may be required to have your high school records and exam results evaluated by an official third party evaluator. (See *Chapter Five – The College Application Process* for details.)

As an American, you are eligible for Federal Aid. The government's Office of Student Aid provides grants, loans and work-study funds for college students under FAFSA (Free Application for Federal Student Aid). The web site – www.fafsa.com, gives detailed information about FAFSA, can estimate your eligibility for federal aid and provides free assistance regarding the form and the aid program itself.

The new government web site – http://studentaid.gov, brings lots of financial advice for students to one portal.

Residency

The term *residency* usually refers to an individual's residency in a particular state in the USA, and is used by colleges to establish whether a student will pay *in-state* or *out-of-state* fees. State residency requirements differ from state to state, but many require you to 'maintain a domicile' in that state for at least 12 months prior to the last day for late registration. In other words your 'constant presence' in that state is required, meaning you cannot leave to go home during that time. Residency cases are decided on an individual basis. Details can be found at – www.collegeboard.com/testing/international/state, together with a list of links to individual states.

High school relationship

Your application to a US college may create extra work for your high school, especially if you are the first student ever to do this. As well as having to send your academic information to each college, many colleges also require two or more letters of recommendation from teachers, and a few request even more information.

According to Clare Brown, Head of Careers at Caterham School in England, non-US teachers, "… are not very good at waxing lyrical about (their) students other than in academic terms; waxing holistically is a new thing."

US colleges expect teachers to write about a student's personality as well as academic performance, so you may need to invest some time in getting the best recommendation letters possible. Tanya Rehki is an Indian student currently studying on the East coast, who remembers, "Our high-school teachers did write some recommendation letters, but our college counselor single handedly had to correct the English of every recommendation letter." If English isn't the first language of your letter writer, try to have someone check the letters before submission. Most college Admissions staff will not hold it against you as long as the meaning of the letter is clear.

Applying to a US college will require assistance from your high school staff so if you're not on good terms with the administration and teachers, you might want to start mending some fences!

Visiting the college

Many American students visit the colleges they're interested in before applying or before accepting an offer. If you're lucky, you'll be able to visit colleges before you decide to apply or accept. If you can't visit, most colleges have brochures for prospective students making every place look like something out of a Hollywood movie.

Consider how you would approach the application process – are you only thinking about one particular college or are you open to anything and everything? The former won't be too much of a challenge, while the latter will take significant time and energy.

Costs

If, like many students, your parents will be paying your fees, discuss the US possibility with them as soon as you can to avoid disappointment. You might not think a few thousand pounds/ dollars/ euros is much in the grand scheme of things, but if your parents are already stretching themselves it could be the deal-breaker. Be sure to discuss realistic figures with them and always include the hidden costs listed below.

Although the financial paperwork required by colleges and the US government only requires proof of funds to cover your first year, the Consular officer in charge of your visa application will often look at the bigger picture and ask not only how you plan to pay for all four years, but also how this will affect the rest of your family.

Fees and financial aid

Although some American college fees are on a par with foreign college rates, many are higher. Unless you have been scouted and offered a scholarship already (which sometimes happens), you should consider how your fees will be paid. There are some need-based and merit-based scholarships* open to foreign students, but this usually depends on the individual college. There is no 'official' national organization to match students with available scholarships, although there are a few private companies who can help for a fee, and a number of web sites that help with the search. When looking at the dollar figures on college web sites, make sure you understand what the amount includes. Some colleges only state tuition fees and others include the cost of housing in the figure. In addition, some colleges charge a 'flat fee', which applies almost regardless of how many classes you take per semester; others charge by the class-load, although international students should remember they are legally required to take a full course-load.

Typically, a college application is based on academics and high school activities – ability to pay doesn't affect your application (called *need-blind*

---

* **Need-based scholarships** are assessed based on family income and the applicant's ability to pay tuition, room and board. Merit-based scholarships are awarded for stellar achievements in areas such as academics, leadership and extra-curricular activities – for these scholarships ability to pay isn't a factor.

applications). This means that while your ability to pay isn't considered, you may receive an offer but no financial aid. There is no US Federal (government) Aid for foreign students, and financial scholarships are thin on the ground compared to those for American/ resident students. Although an F1 visa allows you to work on campus for up to 20 hours per week, foreign students have to prove they can pay a year's fees before being granted a visa. (See *Chapter Four – Funding your College Degree* for details on financial aid.)

Hidden costs

There are a number of costs in the US college application process you might not be aware of:

★ **Applications.** Most colleges charge a fee of between $30 and $100 to submit an application. As many students apply to five or more colleges, this adds up very quickly. Many colleges waive this application fee for students of limited means, so check with the specific college for more details under the 'Admissions' tab on the web site. There are also a few colleges that waive the fee if you apply online – http://www.porcelina.net/freeapps/about.html keeps an updated list of the colleges with free applications. This criterion alone shouldn't decide your choice of college options, but it's worth knowing.

★ **Standardized tests.** The majority of American colleges require test scores from either the ACT or the SAT test. There are fees to sit these tests and additional fees if you're having the scores sent to more than four colleges. If you require your scores to be sent to colleges as soon as possible, rather than within the usual time frame, (called *rush reporting*), this has a higher fee. If you change the place or date of your test you will be charged an additional fee, and there is always a processing fee for international test sitters. Fee waivers exist but these are only available to US citizens. If your first language is not English, you will be required to take an official language proficiency test for which there is a fee. (See *Chapter Five – The College Application Process* and *Chapter Six – Standardized Tests (ACT and SAT)*.)

> ⚠ **WARNING**
> There are hundreds of colleges that don't require ACT or SAT scores from applicants. However, because international students don't have the same academic records as American high school students, these tests scores are an important indicator when considering foreign applications, therefore many colleges require international applicants to take the tests. In some instances an IB or other high school test result may be sufficient, but you should read individual college web site information carefully.

★ **Translation costs.** If your high school information is not in English you must have it translated through a certified transcript translation company, often specified by your college of choice. Some of these companies can give you a price quote very quickly based on the word count of your documents. (See *Chapter Five – The College Application Process* for further details.)

★ **Credential/ transcript evaluation.** While some American colleges are very familiar with foreign academic qualifications and can assess your application themselves, others employ the services of *credential evaluation* or *transcript evaluation* companies to evaluate your high school scores against the American equivalent. (Note *transcript evaluation* and *translation* are **not** the same thing.) Naturally this service is an added, and considerable, expense so find out from each college whether it is necessary. (For more notes on credential evaluations, see *Chapter Five – The College Application Process*.)

★ **Duration.** The majority of undergraduate degree programs in the USA last four years, which adds significantly to the overall cost. You can finish early by taking classes during the summer or loading up your courses, but this may not reduce the cost and you'll still need somewhere to live. If you're only half sold on the idea of spending much more time in higher education, four years as a student is definitely something to think about.

If you're looking for an international experience but not for four years, consider a Study Abroad program from a college in your own country, or an exchange program – http://www.isep.org has a list of US colleges in its directory. WISE (Worldwide International Student Exchange) has comprehensive options for studying abroad.

★ **Non-Immigrant visa.** Once you have accepted the offer of a place you will be applying for a student visa, which costs a substantial amount of money. (See *Chapter Eight – Before You Go – Visa Application and Other Important Steps*, for details of the steps involved for the visa application process, and the US government web site – http://www.uscis.gov for current fees. (Also see *Chapter Five – The College Application Process*.)

★ **Health insurance.** As a student attending an American college, and as a Non-Immigrant visa holder, you will be required to take out health insurance coverage. Annual costs vary depending on the type of coverage you choose, but it is a large expense if you are not currently paying for health care. (See *Chapter Eight – Before You Go – Visa Application and Other Important Steps* for details on health care and coverage.)

Academic considerations

Undergraduate colleges in the USA publish their minimum academic criteria for admission (Grade Point Average and standardized test scores), and all applicants should ensure they meet or exceed these requirements. The general Admissions information will include detailed US high school credit requirements, which will be both confusing and inapplicable to foreign applicants. If there is a specific link for International Applicants on a college Admissions web page, head straight to that link. The 'International' tab will clearly state what is required of you and will give minimum requirements for foreign qualifications:

★ The University of Cambridge International Examinations board (CIE) has a list of worldwide universities that recognize their exams, although it is not exhaustive – http://recognition.cie.org.uk. Similarly, the International Baccalaureate web site shows which US colleges will accept predicted grades, which colleges will give credit for IB results and what the minimum score requirements are – www.ib.org.

★ While many colleges will look at your predicted grades closely, most will also ask for ACT or SAT scores. Visit individual college web sites for further information, as acceptance policies differ. (See *Chapter Six – Standardized Tests (ACT and SAT)* for details on both tests.)

 TIP
There is a practice in some schools to predict lower grades than are expected as a way of keeping students motivated. According to Julia Douglas, Head of US University Applications, Sevenoaks School, England, "If you're marked down in your mocks or midterms, don't panic. Have your school send a letter explaining the situation."

Course work

The American system leaves you very much in charge of your own syllabus and course load. In some education systems, such as that in England, you may decide to study English or History and much of the course is predetermined and restricted to that subject. An American college will require you to put your own schedule together and you are expected to continue studying subjects you have neither interest in, nor talent for. For some students this means picking up a Science or a Language class after a gap of more than three years. (Don't worry, colleges have introductory classes which start from scratch.)

In addition to having to take a Math and Science class when all you want to study is Shakespeare, you will also have to figure out how many of these courses are necessary before you're off the hook, how to get yourself registered, and whether or not you're fulfilling the minimum number of credit hours for your semester. *And* you'll have to do this every semester. You don't just sign up for a four-year degree course and turn up on day one. (See *Chapter Eight – Before You Go – Visa Application and Other Important Steps* for further details.)

On the other hand, the breadth of subjects required by most American colleges is the attraction for some students coming to the USA to study. If you aren't ready to start narrowing down your academic options, or simply love to study in a range of areas, the American college system would be very suitable for you.

Sounds complicated, and it is if you've never experienced this type of system before. Fortunately, most colleges hold separate and thorough orientations for foreign students, and there is a team of staff to support foreign students, as well as academic advisors for all students. (See *Chapter Eight – Before You Go – Visa Application and Other Important Steps* for more information.)

The grading system

Although American college students have final and midterm exams, their course work is also monitored and graded throughout the academic year, as is participation and attendance at many colleges. These grades make up their GPA (Grade Point Average), so if you don't apply yourself at all times, you don't do very well.

The teaching style

US colleges typically do not teach via lectures supplemented by smaller group sessions (tutorials). For most classes, students attend lectures and are given homework assignments. If the class is small enough discussion is encouraged and you will have an opportunity to clear up confusion and ask questions. In large classes there are often hundreds of students in the room or lecture theater, and if you don't understand something it is your responsibility to seek help either from the professor or the TA (teaching assistant).

Academic pressure

If you haven't yet finished high school think carefully about when you would apply to a US college. The application process can be stressful and time-consuming and might be too much to handle along with your final exams. As most US colleges require ACT or SAT scores, this means you have to take them before you can apply anywhere, which in turn means taking them when you are also taking high school exams. As these tests are very different from what you may be used to, they might require months of extra study and perhaps tuition before you are ready to take them. Some foreign students take a year off after high school and apply to US colleges then.

Geographic and cultural considerations

Although you'll probably have a ball while at college in the USA, you will also be a long way from home, family, friends and all that is familiar. As any expat will tell you, this can take its toll.

Distance

American students will probably leave campus for Thanksgiving (in November) and spring break for example, but if you have already flown home for the winter break and have another flight to pay for at each end of the summer, your travel coffers may be empty. Although this doesn't seem to put many international students off, it is definitely something to bear in mind, especially if you're a real home bird.

Language

Even if you speak English, American English has its own peculiarities and vocabulary. Although writing papers and taking tests won't be quite the challenge it is for non-English-speaking students, there is definitely a learning curve ahead. Foreign speaking students need to be able to take classes and write papers in American English. Many American universities require non-English speakers to pass an English language test for admission, but they have large departments devoted solely to supporting their international student body, including language needs.

Culture

Cultural differences are a major factor for foreign students. Again, even if you think you come from a similar background (i.e. the UK), think again. Student life in the USA is very different – the legal drinking age in the country is 21, so there are no student bars on campus. Local bars will *card* you (i.e. ask for proof of age) and refuse under-21s alcohol. Being caught drinking underage anywhere could result in disciplinary and/ or legal action, which in turn could result in the loss of your student visa and deportation at your own expense. According to Rendy Schrader, Director, International Students and Scholars Advising, Indiana University, "British and Canadian students often experience more culture shock because they did not anticipate having any problems at all."

If nothing in this chapter has put you off, you're now ready for the following chapters, which deal with the above topics in more detail.

Chapter Two
An Overview of US Colleges

As American college application forms will contain many unfamiliar words and phrases, this chapter gives a general overview to simplify matters and avoid confusion when applying. More detailed college definitions are given in the relevant chapters following this chapter.

Jargon you'll come across

Although many words and phrases are common to all American colleges, you will come across college-specific jargon. If you're browsing a college web site, but not really serious about that particular college, don't worry too much about understanding or memorizing the jargon. With a college of interest you should spend a little time familiarizing yourself with their vocabulary, so you understand what the college offers and whether it's a fit for you. If you are invited to interview as part of your application, make sure you are familiar enough to converse in the jargon if need be, particularly when it relates to an area of interest to you. For example, if there is a nickname or acronym for the school or department you are applying to, you should know it.

General college jargon

Some jargon is common to most colleges in the USA and you will see the words and phrases as soon as you begin your research:

★ One of the first pieces of jargon you'll hear is the word *app*, – the abbreviation for an *application* to college. The phrase *college apps* is everywhere – if you see *Common App* it refers to a multi-college application process. (Both are covered in detail in *Chapter Five – The College Application Process*.)

★ Another word you'll come across immediately is *Admissions*, which refers to the college office or department dealing with applications from students like you.

★ American high school students are advised by *college counselors* – it the staff member advising on colleges at your school is called a *careers* officer or advisor, US colleges may not understand the term if you use it.

★ Most colleges have an office devoted to supporting international students. These are often called the ISO (International Students Office) or the OISS (Office of International Students and Scholars). Names and abbreviations vary, but you will come into contact with this office as soon as you accept a college offer, and usually before then.

★ On many college web sites, when discussing applications and admissions, you'll see the words *freshmen* and *transfer students*. If you have just finished high school (or the equivalent) and have never attended a degree college before, you will be classed as a freshman applicant. Students who are switching from one college to another are referred to as transfer applicants.

★ Americans tend not to differentiate between colleges and universities in conversation, but there is a difference. A *college* refers to undergraduate higher education only (i.e. a Bachelor's degree) while a *university* includes both undergraduate and postgraduate studies. So for example, within Harvard University, there is Harvard College.

★ The *Ivy League* refers to what are considered the top echelon of US colleges. The Ivy League consists of Brown University, Columbia University, Cornell University, Dartmouth College, Harvard University, Princeton University, University of Pennsylvania, and Yale University.

★ *Varsity* is the word used for sports and other teams that represent the college against other colleges.

★ Perhaps most confusing, the majority of Americans talk about 'school' when they mean university or college. Americans will ask each other where they went to school and they're not usually talking about high school or earlier. (If they wanted to ask about high school specifically, they'd say 'high school'.)

In this book, the word 'college' will be used for all institutions of higher education, unless otherwise stated.

Admissions

This is the term generally used for the department that handles applications and makes offers. Most college web sites have a tab devoted specifically to *Admissions* – all information regarding the application process and academic requirements for the college will be found here. This information is usually split into *undergraduate*, *graduate* and *transfer* sections, so make sure you click on the correct link. Within the *Admissions* section there is usually specific information for international students.

APs

Advanced Placements (APs) are classes and exams US high school students can take in addition to the regular syllabus and the ACT or SAT exams. Applicants are given extra credit with Admissions departments if they have AP credits, but international applicants are usually not expected to have them.

International Baccalaureate

The IB is an academic program (including examinations), taken in high school in some countries but is not the norm in the USA. However, the IB is usually given consideration by colleges when looking at foreign applications. High IB scores may also allow you to skip a few introductory classes – see individual college Admissions pages for more information.

Terminology

There are usually four years of study at American undergraduate degree colleges, and the names of each of these years may not be familiar to you. First year, second year and so on, isn't used in the States. Instead, a first year student is a *freshman*, a second year student is a *sophomore* (pronounced 'soffmore'), in the third year you're a *junior* and in your final year, a *senior*. In between any of these (usually in the summer), you're termed a *rising* sophomore, junior or senior. Additionally, juniors and seniors (in both high school and college) are referred to as upper classmen, while freshmen and sophomores are referred to as lower/ under classmen.

 TIP

Students educated in the British system should note that although a first year student is called a freshman, the term 'fresher' isn't as prevalent as in the UK, and the first week of college isn't referred to as Freshers' Week.

Abbreviations

ACT	–	formerly known as American College Testing, ACT is now the name given to one type of pre-college standardized testing
AP	–	Advanced Placement
DHS	–	Department of Homeland Security
DOS	–	Department of State
DSO	–	Designated School Official
DS -160	–	US Non-Immigrant Visa Application form
FAO	–	Financial Aid Office
GPA	–	Grade Point Average
IB	–	International Baccalaureate
ICE	–	Immigration and Customs Enforcement
IRS	–	Internal Revenue Service
ISO	–	International Student Office
NACAC	–	National Association for College Admission Counseling
OISS	–	Office of International Students and Scholars
OPE	–	Office of Postsecondary Education
RA	–	Residents Assistant
SAT	–	formerly known as the Scholastic Aptitude Test, the SAT is now the name given to one type of pre-college standardized testing
SEVIS	–	Student and Exchange Visitor Information System (Internet-based)
SEVP	–	Student and Exchange Visitor Program
STEM	–	Science, Technology, Engineering and Math
TA	–	Teaching Assistant
USCIS	–	US Citizenship and Immigration Services

Types of colleges

Most foreigners wishing to study at undergraduate level in the USA will be looking at a four-year degree program, referred to as a

Bachelor's degree, which they will obtain at a *college* or *undergraduate college*. Any institutions teaching at postgraduate level are referred to as *grad* (graduate) school and more specifically as Law School, Med School, Business School and so on.

Community college

These are colleges offering two-year *Associate degrees*, as well as diplomas and other technical qualifications – they do **not** offer Bachelors degrees. Formerly called Junior colleges, Community colleges are also known as *tech* and *city* colleges. Many students transfer into the final two years of a four-year degree program elsewhere after gaining their Associates degree at a Community college, so this is definitely an option for international students. Fees are almost always less expensive, so this is becoming an increasingly attractive study path:

★ The US Department of Education has a list of accredited Community colleges on its web site – http://ope.ed.gov/accreditation/.

★ Community colleges generally have an 'open door' admissions policy and only require High School graduation. However, policies vary and you may need to provide transcripts and test scores.

★ Policies and fees for admitting nonresidents (including foreign students) differ from college to college so check individual web sites.

★ Many have *articulation* agreements with undergraduate colleges, whereby their two-year courses are compatible with the requirements of the four-year degree program, and facilitate a fairly smooth transfer onto four-year programs.

★ As you still require an F1, Non-Immigrant visa to attend Community colleges, the visa application process and requirements are the same as for a regular four-year college.

★ Student housing is generally not provided by Community colleges, although they do have staff to assist in finding accommodation, and there are often 'house-stay' options available.

📖 FURTHER READING
See the American Association of Community Colleges for more information on this option – www.aacc.nche.edu.

Public and private colleges

There are public and private colleges in the US, but few of them are free, although some colleges do award prospective students a *full ride*, meaning their tuition, room and board fees are all paid by the college:

★ **Public colleges** are owned by the state they're located in and receive partial funding from that state. They tend to charge students from other states higher fees than their own *in-state* students. Some states have several public colleges. A common practice in larger states is to have branches (*campuses*) of the state university throughout the state, as with Texas, which has nine public universities under the University of Texas umbrella. (University of Texas at Austin, Dallas or at El Paso, for example.)

★ **Private universities** receive no state funds, although most are registered charities (non-profits) and are therefore eligible for tax breaks. Typically, private college fees are higher than public fees, but this isn't always the case.

Both public and private colleges can have endowment funds, meaning money in the bank donated by former students, other charities, and corporations. Where there is a large endowment fund, there is often a larger pot for scholarships. The USA's 'top' colleges are both public and private so do not get distracted by this when narrowing down your choices.

📖 **FURTHER READING**
For a more detailed explanation of the pros and cons of public and private colleges, go to – http://www. parentsandcolleges.com/college-planning/article-02/.

Liberal Arts colleges

You'll hear a lot of colleges described as *Liberal Arts* colleges, which doesn't mean the students all wield paintbrushes. The term is used to describe undergraduate colleges offering a general, rounded curriculum, as opposed to a more technical or vocational education. Typically they are fairly small establishments and students will study a wide variety of subjects for two years before concentrating on their major.

If you don't know your intended major when applying to colleges, most will enroll you in their equivalent of the Liberal Arts school where you will take your 'Gen Ed' (General Education) classes, or core classes. In many colleges this is the School of Arts and Sciences.

Degrees and classes of degree

As an undergraduate you will be studying for a Bachelors degree, although it is not automatically an honors degree. Your Bachelors degree may be a BA (Bachelor of Arts), a BS (Bachelor of Science), a BComm (Bachelor of Commerce), a BFA (Bachelor of Fine Art), a BBA (Bachelor of Business Administration) or a degree specific to your college. In addition, you may achieve a BA in History, English or Journalism for example.

Honors degrees are conferred on students in the top percentiles of their graduating classes. The phrase *in cursu honorum* will appear on both the college transcript and the diploma. In some colleges, you will automatically be considered for an honors degree if your grades are good enough, and in others you must apply for a place on the honors program. (See below for more information on honors programs.)

In addition, students can graduate *cum laude* (with honor or praise), *magna cum laude* (with great honor), or *summa cum laude* (with highest honor). In rare circumstances, a graduate may even receive a *maxima cum laude* degree (maximal honor).

General college information

Academic calendar

Many American colleges employ the semester system, whereby the academic year consists of two semesters with an optional summer semester. The first semester runs from August to December, and the second from January to some time in May. A few colleges have the trimester system, which divides the academic year into three. A small number of colleges run on the quarter system, with three ten-week quarters from August/September to the following May/June, and an optional summer session. The word 'term' is often used interchangeably with semester, trimester or quarter. Classes begin in August although colleges usually have a second (smaller) freshmen intake in January of the following year.

✔ **TIP**
When trying to plan either an application or travel, note that American colleges typically start some time in August, early September at the latest.

Academic curriculum

It surprises many foreign students to learn that a typical American undergraduate degree course requires students to continue to study a wide range of subjects. In your first two years at least, you will probably be taking classes in Science, English, History, Languages and Arts. The good news is there are a large variety of classes within each category so your options are usually good.

Classes and courses

Although you will hear the word courses, you will be said to be taking classes. 'I have a class at nine o'clock on Friday mornings' is a frequently heard complaint among undergraduates:

★ **Core courses** refers to classes undergraduates are required to take before starting their major classes (the subject they want to study in depth).

★ **Distribution Requirements** is another term referring to classes all undergraduates are required to pass.

★ **Gen Ed** (General Education) is the term for the core curriculum most colleges require of their undergraduates.

★ **Electives** refers to classes that are not general requirements but which you can 'elect' to study as part of your degree. (See *Chapter Eight – Before You Go – Visa Application and Other Important Steps* for complete details.)

Credits, or credit hours

American higher education institutions use the credit system. Colleges state a total number of credits, or credit hours, you must achieve in order to graduate, and each class you complete gains you a number of these credits. A four-year undergraduate degree course usually requires 128 credits. This breaks down to 16 credits per semester, or 32 per year, which most colleges consider a *full course load*. (See *Chapter Eight – Before You Go – Visa Application and Other Important Steps* for details.) Once you have a place at a US college look more closely at the graduation credit hour requirements, as they aren't all the same.

Remember that to remain *in status* as an F1 visa holder, you must be enrolled as a full-time student. College ISOs (International Students Office) are informed of your course load and are required to disclose to the US government any students who are not enrolled full-time. In some cases it is possible to take more than the average number of credits, but this usually requires permission from an academic advisor or the relevant professor.

'Class of…'

You will hear and see this phrase frequently in an American college, or you'll see a year in parenthesis after someone's name, e.g. 2015. Both refer to the individual's year of graduation. American students are very proud of their graduation year (from both high school and college), with many schools and college kids having slogans and chants for their particular year. For example, students graduating in 2014 may have 'One Four, Watch us Roar', and many graduates of 2012 had slogans such as 'You can't out-do the class of One-Two'.

Campus

Campus refers to the land or property owned by the college, whether it's in the middle of nowhere or in the center of a large city. Unlike some older British urban colleges, which often have buildings and housing scattered all over a city, urban American colleges tend to have a distinct campus feel to them, mainly because they own large chunks of land in the same area. Student housing is often across the street from the academic buildings. Very large colleges will have several campuses, either in the same city or miles apart throughout the state. Penn State, for example, has 19 campuses, scattered throughout the state of Pennsylvania.

GPA

GPA stands for Grade Point Average and refers to the average grade high school and college students earn over their academic careers. The GPA comes from homework and class assignment grades as well as test scores. Most colleges look closely at a high school student's GPA when considering their applications.

Graduate-level only

There are a few degrees you will not be able to obtain at the undergraduate level – Law being the most different from some other countries, such as the UK. While you can take classes in many areas of Law/ Jurisprudence at American colleges, the Law degree itself is a three-year postgraduate course at Law School. If you are considering a legal career in the USA, there are usually no specific undergraduate majors required for Law School.

Students wishing to become medical doctors must also attend Medical School where they will study a further four years after their undergraduate degree. (Some Medical Schools offer an accelerated seven-year program, combining three years of undergraduate training and four years' postgraduate.) Unlike Law degree candidates, Medical Schools have very specific undergraduate requirements, such as Science, Statistics, Calculus, Humanities and/ or English.

Applicants for Law School and Medical School must also pass the LSAT (Law School Admissions Test) and MCAT (Medical College Admissions Test) respectively.

Honors programs

Many colleges have honors programs or honors societies to recognize excellence in outstanding students. Most honors programs offer smaller classes taught by well-known faculty, with the opportunity to study subjects in more depth. Honors programs at larger colleges offer their students what they might otherwise only get at smaller, Liberal Arts colleges. The programs differ from college to college – some are by invitation only and others you may apply to. In some colleges you are automatically included on the honors program if your academic credentials are high enough. Being an honors student has some prestige, so if you are really keen on this, make sure you look for the options when looking at colleges. There are also scholarships available from many honors societies. (See *Chapter Ten – US College Life – The Lowdown* for more details.)

Majors and minors

A major is the subject you will specialize in e.g. History, Engineering, Bio-Chemistry. Most undergraduate students don't have to declare their majors until they're going into their junior (third) year – they will usually have to complete a series of core classes before being allowed to begin their major. If you are very interested in two disciplines, you can add a minor subject to your degree classification giving you a degree in say, Marketing, with a minor in Humanities, or Music. The two subjects need not be related. Although you are required to declare a major at some point, there is no requirement to declare a minor.

You can also 'double major', meaning you're effectively taking two degrees. You may not have to double up your core classes if both majors have the same requirements, but you will have to complete the required amount of classes to graduate in both disciplines. Not for the faint of heart! Students interested in more than one subject, but unwilling to take on a double major, often declare a minor instead.

Residency

On college applications, *residency* usually refers to the place where you have your permanent domicile. You will see the word frequently because many colleges have different tuition rates for residents and nonresidents, also referred to as *in-state* and *out-of-state* applicants. Residency rules and requirements differ from state to state, but you usually have to have remained in the state for a year to establish residency, meaning you cannot leave during breaks and summer. A number of American students do this and may suggest you can too, however as a non-US citizen the path to residency isn't as simple as staying in one place for a year.

Scholarships, grants, loans and financial aid

As mentioned throughout this book, American colleges often have money to offer in financial aid. As a non-US citizen you will not be eligible for federal grant money from the US government:

★ **Scholarships** do not have to be repaid like loans. They can be *need-based*, where your family's income is considered eligible for financial aid, or *merit-based*, where you are awarded for academic or other qualities. Although most colleges award scholarships in some form, there are many other sources of scholarship money ranging from private charitable organizations, to commercial companies and international agencies. Often scholarships are awarded for every year of the degree program.

★ **Grants** are also gifts of money that do not have to be repaid, and are often awarded on the same basis as scholarships. Grants tend to be a one-time affair, meaning you only receive a sum of money once in your academic career unless you successfully re-apply.

★ **Loans** are sums of money that have to be repaid in some way. As a non-US citizen you won't be eligible for federal loans (i.e. from the

US government), and although US banks offer student loans, they typically only allow international students to take out loans when there is a US citizen to sponsor them.

See *Chapter Four – Funding your College Degree* for more details on financial aid.

Standardized tests

Most colleges ask for scores from standardized tests as a way of measuring applicants against each other. These tests are usually required of foreign applicants so the colleges can compare them against the US applicant pool. Standardized tests include the pre-college ACT and SAT academic tests, as well as language proficiency tests such as TOEFL. (See *Chapter Five –The College Application Process* and *Chapter Six – Standardized Test (ACT and SAT)* for further, comprehensive information.)

Subject abbreviations

College students often abbreviate the names of classes they are taking, so if you listen to any videos on college web sites you might hear:

Anthro	–	Anthropology
Bio	–	Biology
Bio-Chem	–	Bio-Chemisty
Chem	–	Chemistry
Comp-Sci	–	Computer Science
Gen Ed	–	General Education (refers to the core classes students are required to take)
Nut-Sci	–	Nutritional Science
Poly-Sci	–	Political Science
Psych	–	Psychology
Stats	–	Statistics
STEM	–	Science, Technology, Engineering and Math

Fraternities and sororities

Most colleges have fraternities and sororities, which are mainly social organizations for undergraduates. They are usually single sex, *fraternity* being for males and *sorority* for females – some are mixed and are called *co-ed fraternities*. Membership is never mandatory – some colleges have a very high percentage of students belonging to them, while at other colleges they are almost non-existent. Frats and sororities are usually named as combinations of letters of the Greek alphabet, so you'll hear about the Tri-Delts, (Delta, Delta, Delta), and the Phi Delts (Phi Delta Theta), among others. Most are national organizations and are found in many colleges. As well as the social organizations, there are also Professional, Service and Honors fraternities, which are governed by different bodies and have their own rules regarding eligibility and membership.

It is very common for students to wait until their second semester or second year to join a fraternity or sorority, so there's no hurry to do so and I advise you not to let this further complicate your decision-making. (See *Chapter Nine – On Arrival*, for more information.)

Geography

Most states have several colleges and some have very similar names. The University of Oklahoma is not the same as Oklahoma State University and Michigan State is not the same as the University of Michigan. To add to your confusion colleges are often referred to by initials, so the University of Oklahoma becomes OU but the University of Michigan remains simply 'Michigan' (pronounced Mi<u>sh</u>igan). BU stands for Boston University (there is no University of Boston), and there is also a Boston College. There are no rules to these nomenclatures – you'll just have to learn as you go along.

Here are some of the more common abbreviations for American colleges and universities:

A & M	–	Texas A & M University (Agricultural and Mechanical)
ASU	–	Arizona State University
BC	–	Boston College
BMC	–	Bryn Mawr College (pronounced *Brin Mah*)
BU	–	Boston University
BYU	–	Brigham Young University
CU	–	University of Colorado
FSU	–	Florida State University
GW	–	George Washington University
IIT	–	Illinois Institute of Technology
KSU	–	Kansas State University
KU	–	University of Kansas
LSU	–	Louisiana State University
MIT	–	Massachusetts Institute of Technology
NYU	–	New York University
OU	–	Oklahoma University, Ohio University
OSU	–	Ohio State University
RIT	–	Rochester Institute of Technology
SMU	–	Southern Methodist University
SUNY	–	State University of New York
TAMU	–	Texas A & M University
TCU	–	Texas Christian University
TTU	–	Texas Tech University
UCD	–	University of Colorado at Denver
UCLA	–	University of California at Los Angeles
UIC	–	University of Illinois at Chicago
USC	–	University of Southern California
UT	–	University of Texas
UTA	–	University of Texas at Austin
UTEP	–	University of Texas at El Paso
W&M	–	College of William and Mary

Some colleges also have well-known nicknames:

Air Force	–	US Air Force Academy
Annapolis	–	US Naval Academy
Army	–	US Military Academy
Berkeley	–	the University of California, Berkeley
Cal	–	University of California, Berkeley
Caltech	–	California Institute of Technology
Cal State	–	University of California at…
Chapel Hill	–	University of North Carolina at Chapel Hill
Georgia Tech	–	Georgia Institute of Technology
Mizzou	–	University of Missouri
Navy	–	US Naval Academy
Ole Miss	–	University of Mississippi
Oxy	–	Occidental College
Penn	–	University of Pennsylvania
Penn State	–	Pennsylvania State University
Umass	–	University of Massachusetts, Amherst

(pronounced *You-mass*)

Virginia Tech	–	Virginia Polytechnic Institute and State University
WashU	–	Washington University in St. Louis (pronounced Lewis)
West Point	–	the US Military Academy

Most colleges have several sports teams, all of which have nicknames too. For the purposes of your application this is not required information unless you hope to be a student athlete.

BEWARE – degree/ diploma mills

During your Internet searches you will undoubtedly come across *institutions* offering degrees that can be completed in a short time. Although they are usually advertising online studying, they can be confusing to the uninitiated. This is where that old adage applies – *'If it looks too good to be true, it probably is'*:

★ Whenever you read '*Complete your degree in next to no time*', '*Worry-free degrees*' or '*Life Experience Degrees*', you are reading about fake degrees/ diplomas or degrees that are not from accredited establishments.

★ If a college on the Internet sounds strikingly similar to a very prestigious college, you should be on your guard. Remember many American colleges can sound confusingly similar to foreigners, e.g. Miami University and University of Miami are two different establishments, the former not even in Florida.

★ The college may claim to be accredited, but the accreditation board may be a *dummy* or not generally recognized.

★ If the only address given is a PO Box number, it is almost certainly not a *real* college or university.

★ Because it's domain name ends with 'edu' doesn't mean it's a bona fide education establishment.

★ If there are no stated selection criteria, e.g. minimum GPA requirement, it's probably not a *real* college. (Community colleges are the exception, as they generally don't state a required GPA.)

To ensure 'your' colleges are the real thing, check their web sites thoroughly. It's not enough to have glossy-looking photos, although the scam colleges often have very little information on the home page. Check whether they are accredited and then do a check on the accrediting body.

📖 **FURTHER READING**
The US Department of Education has a list of Recognized Accrediting Agencies on its web site – http://www2.ed.gov/admins/finaid/accred/index.html.

The Council for Higher Education also has a list of accredited colleges – http://www.chea.org. Make sure the web site of your chosen college/ s can be clicked through to from these web sites.

Chapter Three
What to Consider When Choosing a College

American students typically apply to only a handful or more colleges. Although it's a daunting prospect for them they are obviously somewhat familiar with the US college system, and have an idea which ones are the most difficult to get into, the most popular, and so on. For foreign students, apart from a few big names, in place of familiarity there's a lot of anxiety and it's often difficult to know where to start. There are over four thousand colleges in the USA – this chapter helps you to narrow the field.

Before you start narrowing I encourage you to widen your knowledge of colleges in the USA. Think beyond the big names you might already know – you'll be surprised and impressed. According to Julia Douglas, who oversees US college applications at Sevenoaks School in Kent, England, "Many students only want to apply to the places they've heard of." As these schools are usually the top colleges, and therefore very difficult to get into, she advises looking further afield from the start.

If you know the subject you'd like to study, it's easier to research colleges by subject to make sure you're looking at the right ones.

Students interested in studying Journalism, for example, might find only a few of the 'top schools' on their list, and some of the most respected Journalism schools will come as a surprise.

International Education Consultant, Hamilton Gregg has found, *'Many students feel pressure by parents to only attend the Top 10 or 20 schools without any understanding of what that really means. Even more complicated for them is to understand there are different rankings.'* If you are set on attending a top college and know the subject you'd like to study, make sure those colleges are the best for that subject – www.topuniversities.com gives rankings by subject and course information on universities around the world.

Although US colleges look at an applicant's academic credentials they are also looking for students who will be a good *fit* for them. Hamilton Gregg adds, *'Many families assume "We will apply and get in" forgetting there is actually an admission process where the college is looking to see if the student can, a) make it academically, b) speak enough English to succeed and c) fit into their campus culture.'* It is important you feel you would do well and feel comfortable at the colleges to which you apply – colleges often ask on their application form why you want to study there and why you think you would be a good fit.

📖 FURTHER READING

The US News College Compass tool contains a 'My fit' search engine to help you find the college that's right for you. For a one-time fee you can enter over 20 criteria about yourself and the 'My fit' tool will identify schools that best suit your wants and needs. Visit the web site at – http://www.usnews.com/usnews/store/college_compass.htm?src=wid.

College features

SEVP approved

First and foremost your college must be an SEVP-approved college. (Student and Exchange Visitor Program.) The US Immigration and Customs Enforcement web site gives an up-to-date list of approved schools together with a map showing locations – www.ice.gov/sevis/students. The DHS (Department of Homeland Security) web site also has a list of all SEVP-approved schools – http://studyinthestates.dhs.gov/school-search/.

> **⚠ WARNING**
> In rare cases, a college has appeared to be government-approved because a subsidiary college may have been accredited in previous years. It may also have been granted SEVP approval without the necessary investigations being undertaken thoroughly. A report by the Government Accountability Office (GOA) identified gaps in the SEVP fraud investigation process. When looking at lesser-known colleges, especially those offering fast-track or cheaper 'deals', make sure they are legitimate – http://www.gao.gov/products/GAO-12-572.

International student body

Look at the percentage of international students the college typically admits each year. While the college may be seeking to increase this number, remember the percentage of international students admitted will always be small compared to the number of American students. You might meet the academic requirements, but your chances of being admitted could be small if the college only has a 5% international student body, compared to some who have 10%.

International student presence

Some colleges have very few international students and some have a larger percentage. This information will be immediately accessible on the college web site, if not by actual numbers then by the information and services available. If you know you will need substantial help in completing your college application or applying for your visa, make sure your colleges of interest can offer this.

While you don't want to mix only with students from your home country (what would be the point in studying abroad?), it may be comforting to know there are other non-American students on campus, and the college is used to supporting foreign students in a variety of matters. Many colleges have student associations for specific regions or countries, which you should be able to find on the web sites. Search for 'International' and the relevant office information should pop up first. The Campus Explorer web site offers many types of college searches, including one by international student presence – http://www.campusexplorer.com/college-tips/CDB502DF/College-Planning-for-International-Students/.

 WARNING
If you end up at 'International Studies' this is often an academic department or discipline at the college, and not the 'International Students' page.

In my interview with Mary Beth Marklein, higher education writer for the *USA Today* newspaper, she stressed the importance of making sure your colleges of choice are able to support international students. "International students should recognize that loneliness is possible and you may need support. A college investing heavily in its reputation with foreign students will also invest in the support services it provides to those students."

Size

Some American colleges are enormous and have around 50 thousand students attending. In colleges this size students are often spread over several campuses, but the sheer number usually means bigger lectures and class sizes, which in turn can mean less time with your professor or teaching assistant (TA). This is not always the case but you should check on the web sites for class sizes.

If you have come from a small school, think carefully about whether you want more of the same or something completely different. One of the biggest changes for students from smaller high schools is the degree of difficulty they experience when trying to consult with professors or teaching assistants. However, graduates from small high schools often thrive at larger colleges, so there are no assumptions to be made.

Class size and student/ faculty ratio

Because most undergraduates have the same required core courses (Math, Science and English or Writing) these classes tend to be large, and in some colleges hundreds of students attend in one huge lecture theater. Generally, the bigger the class size, the less participation there is, which might be a pro or a con to you but is definitely something to consider. Being part of a large class may also mean you have less access to the professor should you require any help.

Location

As an international student, you'll probably be flying from home to college. Make sure you find out how far the journey is from the American airport to your college of interest. Some colleges are miles from anywhere, including airports – even if they are near an airport, it may not be an international one, meaning a layover and connecting flight to get home. What will already be a long journey can be doubled, depending on the distance on the ground. Find out if there is public/ organized transportation from the airport to the college.

Another thing to consider when thinking about the location of the campus is how you'll get around once you're there. Many college students have cars but this may not be an option for you. If you're under 25 years old most car rental companies charge an additional fee of $25 per day or more. Check the web site to see whether there is public or college-provided transportation, both around campus and into nearby towns and cities.

Campus setting

Many college web sites have virtual tours online allowing you to get a good feel for the campus if you can't physically visit before applying. As mentioned in *Chapter Two – An Overview of US Colleges*, American college campuses vary greatly. Some are in the middle of large cities, such as Loyola in downtown Chicago, Georgetown in Washington DC and the City University of New York, while others seem to be miles from anywhere. QS' – http://www.topuniversities.com/country-guides/united-states/state-guides gives descriptions of US states plus their top universities and helps you find your perfect state.

⚠️ **WARNING**

Colorado, Michigan, Utah, Virginia and Oregon allow concealed weapons on college campuses. Be aware legislation may change in other states – http://www.ncsl.org/issues-research/educ/guns-on-campus-overview.aspx.

Campus recreation

Some colleges have fancy gyms and lots of opportunities to join informal sports teams or performing arts groups. If you are someone who values this then find out from college web sites what's on offer. Most colleges have numerous clubs and organizations ranging from sport-oriented to very intellectual and others have thriving theater or music cultures.

The off-campus scene

Many US colleges are fairly isolated. There may be a lot happening on campus, but if you're the type who'd want to venture further for entertainment it's worth looking at what's on offer in the surrounding area.

Single sex colleges

There are still a few single sex colleges in the USA, such as Scripps, a college for women in Claremont, California, and Wellesley, an all female college in Massachusetts. If you want a single sex college, your choices will be restricted but such colleges do exist.

Co-ed versus single sex dorms

Co-ed (or co-educational) dorms are becoming increasingly common in the USA. This means guys and girls have rooms in the same Residence Halls, often on the same floor. Co-ed floors often have bathrooms or shower stalls within the bedrooms, but a few will require you to walk along the corridor to use the bathrooms. If this is definitely not for you, but you really like the college, contact the Housing office to find out if you can be given priority in the allocation of residence halls. This would allow you to request single-sex housing. Although it is possible to change your housing arrangement once you're at college, it is stressful to live in a dorm that doesn't suit you and a switch is not guaranteed.

Religious affiliation

There are many colleges in the US that are, or used to be, run by religious organizations. This doesn't necessarily mean you will feel like you're in a seminary or a convent, and in most of these colleges you won't be aware of the religious affiliation. Well-known colleges and universities with a religious name include Southern Methodist University (SMU), Texas Christian University (TCU), De Paul University, and the various Loyola Universities around the country. There are a few institutions where there is a strong religious element, such as Brigham Young University (BYU) in Utah, which is Mormon. This doesn't mean you have to be Mormon to attend, but a large percentage of students are.

Sports

This can be a big part of student life at American colleges, not only for the athletes but also for most of the students, who follow their teams with passion. Sometimes it seems to border on fanaticism to those of us not brought up with the culture. You will hear reference to *The Big Ten* or *The Big Ten Conference*, which refers to a group of twelve universities tied by their love of sports. (While they are devoted to their sports teams, these institutions also boast high academic standards.) There are many other colleges and conferences around the country with a similar student passion for sports. If you think you can live, eat and sleep college sports, then look at these places, but if you're not at all interested, you might consider a less intense environment. (See *Chapter Ten – US College Life – The Lowdown*, for more on college sports.)

Current and former students

Many colleges have current students as part of their admissions teams and these individuals are available to talk to applicants. In addition to the official voices there are also various web sites where you can chat to students from all over the USA and get the lowdown on colleges, departments and even individual faculty members – www.ratemyprofessors.com is a particularly detailed and informative web site. Most colleges have pages on Facebook where you can ask questions of the current students and talk to other high schoolers who are also applying.

The weather

The USA is vast and the weather varies greatly from one coast to the other. Northern states are often very, very cold in the winter and the winters are long. If you come from a warm country, you probably can't imagine how cold some states can get in the USA. Southern states can be extremely hot and humid in the summer, although as most students aren't at college during this time, it won't be so much of a consideration. If the weather means a lot to you, read more than just the college web site information to make sure you could live in the climate.

Academic standards

Academic averages and requirements

Most colleges state minimum academic requirement for applicants, such as a 3.2 GPA and so on. In addition, many college web sites have a 'Freshman Class Profile' page giving you the average GPA and ACT/SAT test scores of last year's successful applicants. Both should tell you immediately how high the standard is and whether you have a chance of being admitted. If you are applying to a specific school within the college, such as Engineering or Pre-Med, make sure you look at their requirements and averages as they might be higher than the general college numbers. Unless you have a remarkable résumé, your ACT/SAT scores should match, if not exceed, the scores quoted on the web site. Because most colleges admit a limited number of international students, the competition for these places could be very stiff.

📖 **FURTHER READING**

At www.collegedata.com you can calculate your college admissions chances. The College Toolkit web site allows you to search for colleges using your ACT or SAT test scores – http://colleges.collegetoolkit.com/ CommunityToolkit/CanIGetIn/Search/BySATACT.aspx. For a fee, the US News web site breaks down college admissions information by test score requirements, acceptance rate, applicant pool size and so on – http://www.usnews.com/usnews/store/college_compass. htm?src=wid.

Some colleges will list minimum requirements for international students. If you are in a country such as the UK, where many college offers are based on a 'predicted score' at A Level, check specific US college web sites very carefully to see whether they will accept predictions or whether you need actual results. If the information isn't on the web site, call or e-mail the International Admissions Office, as this is crucial information and will obviously affect the timing of your application. (Every British student I have spoken to or about, received offers based on ACT/SAT scores and predicted grades at A level.)

Many colleges require American applicants to have two or three years of a Foreign Language, Math and Science in order to be considered. As foreign high schools don't specifically cater to US college requirements, check to see if your chosen colleges make any exceptions if you don't meet these requirements.

✔ **TIP**

If you feel your academic information can't be communicated on the college app, or the Admissions department in question might not understand your qualifications, don't be afraid to submit an explanation either on the form or in a separate e-mail. Most college Admissions processes can accommodate academic qualifications that are different from those in the US.

Academic credit

Many colleges will give credit (or credit hours) for your international academic qualifications when looking at your application. For example, American students who have taken APs (Advanced Placements) in specific subjects are often able to start a college degree course with a handful of credit hours already under their belt. Many colleges will give similar credit to good A Level results or IB scores. This means when you attend the college you can skip a few classes, and, where colleges bill by the number of classes taken, save some money. (See *Chapter Two – An Overview of US Colleges* and *Chapter Eight – Before You Go – Visa Application and Other Important Steps* for details on credits.)

In colleges where these academic qualifications don't count as extra credit hours, they may still enable you to test out of a few core classes, or to place into a higher-level class in a particular subject. This, in turn, will get your core class requirements out of the way, allowing you to register for electives earlier. Colleges differ in their treatment of AP, IB and other international credentials so check the web sites carefully or call the Admissions office for guidance if this is relevant.

Applications versus offers

The college web site will usually give the ratio of applications to offers accepted, which will give you an idea of the competition you face. Remember, this number usually reflects the total applicant pool, not only international students.

College rankings

Excellence in a particular subject

If you know you want to major in a particular subject (i.e. study the subject in depth), or play a particular sport, look at colleges who claim it as a strength or are recognized for excellence in that field. They may not necessarily be the 'Top 10' colleges. It is sometimes difficult to glean this information from the college's own web site (they're hardly likely to say they're 'just okay' in a certain area). However, other web sites and tables can suggest colleges to look at for different disciplines (see below). Small Liberal Arts colleges tend not to specialize in the Sciences or technical subjects such as Engineering. If you want to concentrate in a specific area, make sure you aren't applying to a college with a completely different specialization. This may look odd on your application and the Admissions office may decide you are not a good fit for their college.

If you are trying to play a particular sport at college level you should first find which colleges might be interested in you. Not all colleges have D1 teams for every sport and you could waste time looking at some great ones only to find they don't have a good soccer/ golf/ fencing program. (D1 is the highest level of collegiate sports – there are also lower D levels, as well as more informal intramural sports.) The college sports scene is very competitive but a phone call direct to the specific college program is often your best source of accurate information, especially for introductory and general questions. (See *Chapter Five – The College Application Process* for more details on sports applications.)

College character and reputation

Many American colleges have a distinct personality and there are league tables to identify them. For example, some colleges are known as party places, others are known for their sports, and some are known to be academically stringent.

Web sites such as the *Princeton Review's* www.thebestcolleges.org and http://www.princetonreview.com/college-rankings.aspx rank colleges using many different criteria. Lists include *Best Party Colleges, Best*

Greek Life, and so on. If you have a specific area of interest, or a criterion important to you in your college search, typing a short phrase into your search bar will bring up numerous lists.

 WARNING

Some college ranking web sites receive payment from the colleges they rank, therefore what they regard as the *top* colleges might not be generally thought of as the best. I would advise searching on at least three of these sites to make sure the *top* colleges appear several times. If a college only appears on one list, visit its web site and do your homework on it.

Costs

Attending a US college is generally not regarded as cheap. The USA's Department of Education web site contains comprehensive information on college costs in the country, presenting it in lists to make comparisons easy – http://collegecost.ed.gov/. Individual college web sites also give details of tuition, room and board fees. In many colleges freshmen and sophomores are required to live on campus, so when looking at board fees make sure you understand what it covers. Also make sure you are looking at *out-of-state* or *nonresident* fees, and at the tuition costs for international students, in case there is a difference.

 WARNING

Don't forget to factor in the cost of living in the location of each college. Big cities will be more expensive than smaller college towns.

Financial aid/ scholarships

If it is important, or essential, you have help in paying college fees, this should be one of your highest search priorities and researched in conjunction with your college searches. There is a lot less money available to foreign students and some colleges offer no funding at all. *Chapter Four – Funding Your College Degree*, is essential reading if you are looking for financial aid.

Work available

Non-Immigrant student visa holders (F1) are allowed to work for pay up to 20 hours per week *on campus* in the freshman year. *On campus* means you must be employed by your college or by a commercial organization serving the college, such as a bookstore. Off campus employment must be educationally affiliated with the college. You may hold more than one job, but your total hours cannot exceed 20. If you need to work to help finance your way through college, the larger the college the more jobs there will be on campus. Each college will have a page on its web site devoted to available job listings and will include a wide range of positions. Check out these pages to get an idea of the job availability at each college. F1 visa holders may start their campus job up to 30 days before classes start.

> ⚠ **WARNING**
>
> A salary from on-campus work is not included in the financial paperwork you are required to submit when you apply. You (or your parents) will still have to prove ability to pay for the first year's tuition, room and board.

See the US government web site for more details on F1 employment – http://www.ice.gov/sevis/employment/faq_f_on1.htm.

50

College Fairs

Attend college fairs in your country if you can – many colleges now send recruiters around the world. However, there are also a growing number of virtual college fairs:

★ **College Week Live** offers free online college fairs and allows you to interact with admissions staff from over three hundred participating US colleges – http://www.collegeweeklive.com/

★ **The EducationUSA** web site has details of international college fairs in your region – www.educationusa.info

★ **The Fulbright Commission** organizes college fairs in London, which are free to attend, and have over 100 US colleges exhibiting – www.usacollegeday.eventbrite.co.uk

★ **The Institute of International Education** (IIE) hosts US college fairs (free to students and families) around the world where you can get information about US colleges, meet admissions staff and college alumni, attend seminars about the colleges and visa requirements – http://www.iie.org

★ **The National Association for College Admission Counseling** (NACAC) has a comprehensive web site giving information on all aspects of college admissions, as well as up to date information on international college fairs – www.nacacnet.org

★ **Hobsons offer virtual college fairs with free sign-up.** You can web chat with college professionals from any Internet connection around the globe – www.hobsonsevents.com

★ **QS' Top University** also holds college fairs all over the world with international colleges exhibiting –www.topuniversities.com/tour

★ **University Fairs** gives an impressive list of college fairs around the world, allowing you to search by country for a fair near you – http://universityfairs.com/

Demonstrated interest

More and more colleges are placing weight on *demonstrated interest* from their applicants, which means they want to hear from you more than once during the application process and be assured of your interest in attending. You can show this interest by visiting the college table or booth at college fairs, visiting the campus, interviewing at the college or with a local representative, e-mailing or phoning with any questions you might have and sending a thank you note after any face-to-face contact. Be careful not to cross the line between contact and harassment.

Web sites

The following web sites will allow you to narrow your college search by choosing from scores of criteria, such as campus size, areas of interest, religious affiliation, scholarship possibilities, hobbies and sports etc. Many allow you to set up a free profile, but I advise against doing this on too many web sites as this will create more confusion and work for you. Once you've looked at the sites, choose a few which appeal to you and work with them:

★ **ACT official web site** – www.act.org
★ **Big Future**, the College Board's web site, offering searches and much more – https://bigfuture.collegeboard.org/college-search
★ **Cappex** – www.cappex.com
★ **College Confidential** – www.collegeconfidential.com
★ **College Data** – www.collegedata.com
★ **College Prowler** – http://collegeprowler.com
★ **College Search** – www.collegesearch.org
★ **College View** – www.collegeview.com

★ **Education USA** – the US government's web site – http://www.educationusa.info
★ **International Student** – www.internationalstudent.com
★ **National Association for College Admission Counseling** – www.nacacnet.org
★ **Peterson's College Search** – www.petersons.com/college-search.aspx
★ **The Princeton Review** – www.princetonreview.com
★ **Student Service Search** – when you register to take a College Board exam (the SAT for example) you can opt into the Student Search Service, whereby your information is passed to colleges who might be interested in you. These colleges will then contact you. The process is strictly governed by the College Boards rules – http://professionals.collegeboard.com/k-12/prepare/sss
★ **US News web site** – http://colleges.usnews.rankingsandreviews.com/best-colleges

✔ **TIP**
Make notes as you read about colleges. This will help if you have to choose between multiple offers later.

If you are interested in a specific subject and are visiting colleges, it's a good idea to ask to speak to a faculty member from that school or department. While they may not always remember your name for the future, it gives you a chance to ask very targeted questions, and is something you can add to your application when it's time to submit it. Be sure to organize this well in advance, as most professors are not available for impromptu visits.

Some colleges specifically state on their web sites that while they welcome phone calls and e-mails, they do not consider demonstrated interest when looking at applicants.

There is a lot to consider when looking at US colleges, so make sure you allow plenty of time for this step in the process. If you really are at a loss in terms of what you want in a college, choose a couple of college web sites and make a note of what you like and dislike as you're reading. Hopefully you'll begin to see a pattern – do you want an urban setting? Is a strong Arts school important? If you can visit a few colleges this will also help you make decisions.

> ⚠ **WARNING**
> Most colleges hold open days throughout the year, consisting of an introductory talk and a campus tour. In most cases this is run by the general Admissions office and is not specific to any particular school or department. If you are interested in a particular school or area of study make sure you arrange to see that school too.

Chapter Four
Funding your College Degree

If you need financial assistance to attend college in the USA you should be looking at funding options as you do your college search, otherwise you may end up with a college offer and no money. This research can be time-consuming and the application procedure lengthy, so remember to factor the time needed into your overall college and application search. This chapter explains the basics of college scholarships and gives many resources to help with your search – sports/ athletic scholarships are covered at the end of the chapter:

★ According to NAFSA (Association of International Educators), in the 2009-2010 academic year over $670,000 international students received more than $7.2 billion collectively in financial aid from American colleges.

★ Unfortunately, the financial aid policies of US colleges differ widely so you cannot escape doing a lot of research. There are a few web sites that will list colleges giving aid to international students (see below), but you will have to visit the individual college web sites for detailed information, unless you are paying a third party consultant or agency to do this for you. If you don't have the means to hire such help it is entirely possible to do the research yourself, but you must give yourself a lot of extra time to do so.

★ If you have specific colleges in mind, go to their web sites to see if you are eligible for financial aid from them. If it's not clear on the web site, phone or e-mail the Admissions or Financial Aid offices. Also ask for suggestions for funding from other sources, as the staff will probably have knowledge of options. Remember, different schools and departments within a college may also award scholarships.

★ There are various types of financial aid available to students, and they can come from government, college or external third-party sources. Financial aid information can usually be found under the 'Admissions' tab, but make sure you search for financial aid information relating specifically to international students, as many colleges make no awards to non-US citizens or green card holders.

★ Take the time to fully understand the college's financial aid policy for international applicants. Sometimes the language is vague and what sounds like a strong likelihood of funding is, in fact, the reverse. If the wording is not clear contact the Admissions office directly with your questions. (See below for different funding options usually offered by colleges.)

★ Many colleges awarding financial aid to international students require applicants to submit a CSS Financial Aid Profile®, which will be linked from their web site. A CSS Profile® is an online application for financial aid – the information is used by many colleges to award non-federal student aid funds. The form is also available at the College Board web site along with instructions on how to complete it. To submit this form, you must first register with the College Board – http://profileonline.collegeboard.com. If the cost of submitting the form is beyond the reach of your family's finances, contact the college's Financial Aid office to discuss sending your information another way.

> ✔ **TIP**
>
> US citizens and green card holders are eligible to apply for federal financial aid (Pell Grants) using the FAFSA form. Detailed information can be found at the government web site – http://studentaid.ed.gov, including all categories of non-US citizens who are eligible. The FAFSA form is also available on individual college web sites.

★ Some colleges will only allow you to apply for financial aid at the time of your initial freshman application, stating that if you might need financial assistance at any time during your four-year degree program, you should apply at the start. This means you will not be considered for financial aid after this point at these colleges, even if your circumstances change.

★ In all cases with financial aid, keep an eye on the application deadlines as they may not be the same as the deadlines for applications to study at the college.

★ Financial aid exceeding the cost of college tuition may be liable for federal and state taxes in the USA. (See *Chapter Ten – US College Life – The Lowdown* for details).

Negotiating your financial aid

As most colleges have control over how much money they award to individual students, it is sometimes possible to negotiate the amount they are offering you. College funding expert Kalman A. Chany* advises that if your family still can't afford for you to attend a college despite its financial aid offer, you should go back to the college and explain your situation. If your circumstances have changed since you

---

* *Paying for College Without Going Broke*, The Princeton Review, Random House Inc., New York, 2012

applied for aid, or if you have additional supporting documentation, let the college's Financial Aid office know.

Another situation where you might have negotiating strength, according to Chany, is if two colleges of interest have offered different financial aid packages and you prefer the college offering the lowest amount. To be successful this negotiating must be done before you accept any offers. If the college really wants you to attend it might match the better offer, but do not lie about your offers.

Chany also warns that applying Early Decision to a college (see *Chapter Five – The College Application Process*) may be a gamble with regard to the financial aid you receive, because you effectively give up your bargaining position by committing to attend.

Scholarships

A *scholarship* means you are given money you are not required to repay. However, with many scholarships you must maintain a certain minimum grade average and it you fall below this grade you may lose the scholarship the following year:

★ Scholarships can be either *need-based* or *merit-based*. Need-based scholarships are means-tested, and you will be required to prove you or your parents do not have the funds to fully cover your college tuition. Merit-based scholarships are awarded for academic excellence, athletic prowess or other non-financial criteria, and are also grade contingent. Some colleges only offer need-based funding and others only confer merit awards, so again, make sure you understand what's on offer before applying.

★ Scholarships can be awarded by colleges or by third party organizations such as charitable foundations or businesses. In some instances the government of your country of origin may award scholarships to students wishing to study overseas, so be sure to search your own government's web sites. A simple Internet search of 'Financial Aid for – students' (inserting your country) will identify grants and scholarships for students of your nationality.

★ According to an article in the US News, (*10 Colleges That Give the Most International Student Financial Aid*, Katy Hopkins, October 16, 2012) nearly 800 colleges made financial awards to international students in the 2010-11 academic year. The colleges reported as awarding the most were:
- Yale University
- Wesleyan University
- Skidmore College
- Amherst College
- Trinity College
- Gettysburg College
- University of Chicago
- Williams College
- Vassar College
- Colby College

> ⚠ **WARNING**
> If you are awarded both a college scholarship and financial aid from another body, you must inform your college of the additional aid. In most cases the college will make amendments to the aid it grants you.

Merit-based scholarships

Some merit-based scholarships are automatic if your application is successful and you are in a high academic percentile. This good news comes with your offer letter, usually from March onwards for a fall semester start. Unfortunately it's not very easy to find out beforehand if you are to be a recipient. Other scholarships (such as honors scholarships or Departmental scholarships) are usually open to everyone, but you may have to apply for them. Again, this information often doesn't come until your offer letter arrives:

★ Because many merit awards aren't decided until March or later (for a fall intake), colleges may not allow financial aid applicants to apply early, or will state that students who apply early will not be eligible for financial aid. (See *Chapter Five – The College Application Process* for details on early applications.)

★ If you have a particular skill or strength in academics, the Arts or a sport, include this in your scholarship search as many college departments award their own scholarships. For example, if you have narrowed your colleges down to a handful and have a particular subject or sport you want to pursue, go to that area or school on the web site to see if they make awards. (See below for more information on athletic scholarships.)

Need-based scholarships

Some US colleges award scholarships and grants to international students who can prove their eligibility for financial aid. Details differ from college to college, but they all require a statement of finances from whoever is going to be paying the college fees.

The following colleges have a *need-blind* admissions policy for all students, including international, and pledge to meet their financial needs to ensure successful applicants are able to attend. In these cases *need-blind* means that inability to pay is not an impediment to admission:

★ **Amherst** – www.amherst.edu. Amherst also provides long and short-term loans to international students.

- ★ **Dartmouth** – www.dartmouth.edu. Dartmouth does not give any merit-based financial aid.
- ★ **Harvard** – www.harvard.edu. Harvard pledges its financial aid policies are the same for US and international applicants.
- ★ **Massachusetts Institute of Technology (MIT)** – http://web.mit.edu. MIT meets the full financial need of all successful applicants.
- ★ **Princeton** – www.princeton.edu. Princeton awards *packages* of financial aid and an on-campus job.
- ★ **Yale** – www.yale.edu. Needs are evaluated taking into account the relative differences between the US economy and that of your home country.

Some colleges are *need-blind* to international students *to the extent that they are able*. This means all international students they admit will be given the financial aid they need and once the money runs out, an international applicant's ability to pay will factor into the admissions decision. In other words, as an international applicant it is advisable to apply as early as you can.

Need-sensitive financial aid

Many colleges are now professing to be *need-sensitive* or *need-aware* to the applications of international students. One such college is the University of Chicago, (U of C), which states: *'If you apply for financial aid and you are offered admission, you will receive a financial award in the form of grants and scholarships that meets your full demonstrated need.'*

The U of C's definition of *need-sensitive* is: *'when reviewing international applications, the U of C takes into account whether or not an applicant has requested financial assistance'* – https://collegeadmissions.uchicago.edu/.

- ★ Unfortunately this type of admissions policy can result in someone being rejected by a college because of his or her inability to pay.

For example, the University of Pennsylvania: *'will not admit a financial aid candidate for whom we cannot provide aid. As a result, some candidates we would otherwise want to admit will be turned away.'* This does not mean you shouldn't apply, but understand your need for financial aid might work against you. The belief behind this approach is colleges would rather not admit students if they (the colleges) cannot meet the students' full financial aid needs.

★ Wesleyan University has recently moved from a *need-blind* admissions policy to a *need-sensitive* policy. Now most student applications will be considered without regard for their financial circumstances, but towards the end of the application period the last 10% or so will have their ability to pay considered as part of their application.

Athletic scholarships

If you are interested in playing sport at college level and are in need of financial aid, you should first ensure you have a thorough understanding of college sports in the USA and of athletics recruitment.

As many college sports programs are governed by the NCAA (**National Collegiate Athletic Association**) visit the web site for an overview of the application procedure, eligibility requirements and the role of the NCAA – http://www.ncaa.org/.

The National Association of Intercollegiate Athletes (NAIA) has almost 300 member colleges, governs 60,000 student athletes playing 13 sports, and claims to give out over $450 million in scholarship money – www.naia.org.

The National Junior College Athletic Association (NJCAA) is the organization governing sports for athletes at two-year, or Community colleges – www.njcaa.org. Also see *Chapter Five – The College Application Process*, which covers college applications.

When researching sports scholarship options remember to make sure you can meet the academic requirements of individual colleges too. You may be good enough in your field of sport, but you'll still have to satisfy the regular Admissions requirements, such as ACT/SAT scores and high school grades:

★ Athletic scholarships are generally for one year, renewable for the four-year duration of your degree course. They can be full or partial, although international students who are scouted by colleges sometimes receive a *full ride*, which means all costs, including airfare home, are covered. Division III college student athletes are not awarded sports scholarships in NCAA member colleges. It is important to know in which division you would play (if applicable), as this will affect your scholarship chances.

★ If you are in need of financial aid for college, it will be virtually impossible to work and play your sport, such are the demands of the training and play schedules. If you want to play and you need extra money, you need to look for financial aid.

★ Because the NCAA and the NAIA dictate how many scholarships colleges can offer, many colleges divide this number into half or quarter scholarships and smaller, to attract more athletes. This means very few athletes get a full ride. Before awarding any financial aid coaches will often direct you to find funding from other sources, such as your school or department within the college.

★ Although there are many recruitment consultants around who specialize in athletics don't sign up with any of them until you know what you can achieve on your own, especially if they are asking for large amounts in fees. If you know the college(s) you'd like to try for, go to their web sites first to see what information is required from sports applicants. Many ask you to contact the specific sports coach directly as your first step.

★ With regard to athletic recruitment in general, you need to do most of the work – college coaches won't come to you. This is in part because the NCAA strictly governs how and when college coaches can communicate with prospective players, whereas applicants and their families aren't under the same restrictions.

★ When you are looking for information relating to playing sports at US colleges, make sure you're not looking at the college's sports web site, as it usually only contains information on its teams, their schedules and their student fans. Go through the Admissions pages first and then search for sports or *Varsity* sports.

★ As many sports scholarships are awarded late in the recruitment process, you are advised to keep looking at other funding options while you pursue your acceptance into a college sports program. If you are offered funding from elsewhere, you must inform your colleges of interest as sports funding is governed by strict rules.

★ If you are offered financial aid as part of a D1 or D2 sports package, the college should not issue your I-20 until you have been certified as a final qualifier (D1) or a partial qualifier (D2) by the NCAA. (Colleges must issue an I-20 to all incoming international students before the visa application process can begin.) If you arrive at college (because it has issued an I-20) and are subsequently judged ineligible by the NCAA, you will be *out of status* and may end up being sent home. (See *Chapter Eight – Before You Go – Visa Application and Other Important Steps*, for comprehensive details.)

★ Don't forget to contact national and local sports associations in your area to see if they award scholarships.

★ The NCAA reports that only about 2% of American high school athletes receive scholarships to play their sport at college. This is a very competitive arena.

> ✔ **TIP**
> Ivy League colleges and universities do not award athletic
> scholarships but might award you regular financial aid
> anyway if they really want you.

The following are web sites help find sports scholarships:

★ www.activerecruiting.com
★ www.berecruited.com
★ www.collegecoachesonline.com
★ www.college-scholarships.com
★ www.collegesportsscholarships.com
★ www.edupass.org
★ www.fastweb.com
★ www.finaid.org
★ www.prepchamps.com
★ www.trupreps.com

Grants

Grants are awards of money you don't have to repay, but they tend
to be a one-time only offer. Many colleges use the terms *grant* and
scholarships interchangeably.

One of the best-known grant-making organizations is Fulbright.
This program offers grants to: '*study, teach and conduct research for
US citizens to go abroad and non-US citizens to come to the USA*'. It
awards around 4000 grants per year to foreign students and operates
in 155 countries. The web site contains individual country pages
where you can look for details of funding and contact information
specific to your country or region – http://fulbright.state.gov. It
is important you look at your country's page, if it is a member country,
as eligibility and grants available differ widely.

Fulbright states it: '...*operates on a yearly application cycle, which generally (but not in all cases) opens approximately 15 months before the anticipated start of the grant with a deadline approximately 11 or 12 months before the grant's start date*'. In other words, this isn't something you can leave till the last minute.

Loans

Loans can either be personal loans or student loans. Non US-citizens are not eligible for US federal student loans with the exceptions stated on the government web site – http://studentaid.ed.gov/eligibility/non-us-citizens. Private banks and financial institutions fund the loans available to international students:

★ Student loans typically require a co-signer who is a US citizen or permanent resident (green card holder) and who has lived in the USA for the previous two years.

★ Many student loans require you to have a place at college and your student visa in-hand before applying. Some students are able to show loan approval as proof of ability to pay college tuition fees when applying to their colleges of choice, but this is up to each individual college. The loan approval may also be taken into account when the visa application is reviewed, but again, this is up to individual embassies or consular officers.

★ Begin by asking your college if it has a preferred lender and then do your homework.

★ Many lenders have a list of *eligible* colleges in the USA. If your college isn't on a lender's lists contact the college directly to see if they have other suggestions or contacts for obtaining student loans.

★ Student loan funds are disbursed directly to the college you are to attend.

★ Most financial and student advisors strongly encourage you to look for scholarships and grants before taking out loans.

Where to search

The following web sites contain information on financial assistance available to international students. Many of these web sites require some specifics such as where in the USA you want to study, or which majors you are interested in studying:

★ **Big Future** is a College Board web site which allows you to search for scholarships using very detailed parameters, including field of academic interest – https://bigfuture.collegeboard.org/scholarship-search.

★ **Campus Explorer** allows you to search for scholarships by major, state or college – www.campusexplorer.com.

★ **College Scholarships** is a searchable database and a source of financial aid itself – www.collegescholarships.org/.

★ **CollegeWeekLive** is a 'free online event' designed to help prospective students. It has regularly updated information on available scholarships too – www.collegeweeklive.com.

★ **Edupass** lists colleges awarding scholarships to international students. It does not include colleges who offer few financial awards, or colleges that award sports scholarships to international students –http://www.edupass.org/finaid/undergraduate.phtml.

★ **International Financial Aid and College Scholarship Search** gives information on scholarships, grants and loans, together with a loan comparison tool – http://www.iefa.org.

★ **The International Students Office** (ISO) Has a list of scholarships and grants on its web site – http://www.isoa.org/list_scholarships.aspx.

★ **International Student** offers a study abroad and student scholarship search by country, field of study or by chosen university. Also gives information on loans – www.internationalstudent.com/scholarships.

★ **The Institute of International Education** (IIE) has a comprehensive list of financial assistance available to foreign students coming to the USA to study – http://www.iie.org/en/What-We-Do/Fellowship-And-Scholarship-Management.

★ **International Baccalaureate** lists worldwide scholarships available for holders of the IB – http://www.ibo.org/diploma/recognition/scholarships/.

★ **International financial aid and college scholarship search** – http://www.iefa.org/.

★ **International Student Loan** is part of the International Student Network. Colleges must be listed as *eligible* – http://www.internationalstudentloan.com.

★ **Scholarships 4 Development** has a link to many US colleges offering financial aid to international students from developing countries. They stress this is a list-only web site and they do not offer one-on-one advice or processing services – http://www.scholars4dev.com/6499/scholarships-in-usa-for-international-students/.

★ **Questbridge** connects '*the world's brightest low-income students to American's best universities and opportunities*'. The free application links you to numerous quality US colleges and helps match you to full scholarships – http://questbridge.org. Not all partner colleges

will consider international applicants but the following are stated as doing so, and the list is constantly being revised:
- Brown
- Carleton
- Grinnell
- Princeton
- Swarthmore
- Tufts
- University of Chicago
- Washington and Lee
- Yale

★ **United States Student Achievers Program** currently has programs in 16 countries on four continents where USAP: '*offers students material and information resources to enable them to apply to colleges where they otherwise would not have the opportunity or means to do so.*' USAP does not grant scholarships but works with its students to access information to help obtain financial aid, as well as giving support through the college application and visa processes – www.usapglobal.org.

Scams

In your research you will come across promises of scholarship money that seem too good to be true, and they usually are. There are legitimate companies promising to find you scholarship money, but there are many companies who will ask for a *processing fee* or other money up front and then you won't hear from them again. To guard against such scams:

★ Do not forward a *monetary processing fee*. Even if the company pays out a few $1,000 scholarships, there are usually so many applicants your chances of being awarded one are low.

★ Anyone *guaranteeing* scholarship money should be a red flag to you. Even if they say they'll refund your money if they don't find a match, there's a high possibility you won't see it again.

★ Similarly, if you've been told you've won a scholarship you didn't apply for, it's probably not going to materialize even for a small fee. It doesn't make sense that companies are seeking you out to give you money.

★ If you attend seminars on scholarships and student loans they may be thinly disguised sales promotions, trying to get you to sign up for something that will cost you money.

★ Do your homework and check with the Better Business Bureau – www.bbb.org to see if these companies have any complaints against them. Google the company to see if scams have been reported.

★ Loan scams offering ridiculously low interest rates should make you think twice, especially if they ask for a small fee upfront.

Affordable studying in the USA

Another way of being able to afford to study in the USA is to look for colleges with low tuition rates. When you look at the numbers make sure you know what you're looking at. Some colleges state only tuition fees while others include room, board, books and other expenses. Make sure you are looking at *out-of-state* tuition rates. Many colleges have much lower rates for students who are resident in that state – *residency* means a student's permanent domicile is in that state:

★ Web sites such as College Stats give lists of the lowest tuition fees for out-of-state students – http://collegestats.org/colleges/all/lowest-outofstate-cost.

★ The US government web site allowing you to research costs by college – www.collegecost.ed.gov.

★ Kiplinger also has its *Best Value in Public Colleges* list, which gives an extensive list of colleges and detailed statistics on each individual college – www.kiplinger.com/tools/colleges/. Although many of the colleges award large amounts in financial aid, it is mainly to in-state applicants and/ or US citizens.

If you are interested in a particular college on this list, it is definitely worth visiting the web site and looking carefully through the scholarships and grants on offer. For example, the University of Georgia at Athens (UGA) awards many scholarships and not all require US citizenship. One in particular, the Classic City Scholars award, grants two annual scholarships to two Year 13 graduates from secondary schools in Oxford, England. In 2012, the minimum amount of this award was $18,210 and the scholarship is renewable every year for the four years – https://www.admissions.uga.edu/article/scholarships-at-uga.html.

★ Don't forget about Community colleges (see *Chapter Two – An Overview of US Colleges* for details). They are becoming increasingly recognized as a more affordable way for international students to begin studying in the USA. Many good Community colleges have guaranteed acceptance agreements with local four-year colleges. If you know which geographical area in the USA you'd like to study in, consider that state's Community colleges for your first two years.

★ Your own country's colleges might have campuses in the USA or exchange agreements with universities in the USA. Investigate these options as the fees might be cheaper.

★ CLEP – as mentioned in *Chapter Seven – Offers and Rejections*, you may be able to take online tests for college credit. CLEP is the College-Level Examination Program run by the College Board (who also administer the SAT test) – http://clep.collegeboard.org/. For a much smaller fee than a semester's tuition you can take one of a variety of CLEP tests and gain hours of college credits. Don't take any CLEP exams until you have established their worth at your colleges of interest. Some colleges do not give credit for classes not taken on their own campus.

★ EducationUSA, the US Department of State's advising network has advising centers in 170 countries offering free help to international students to find the school that's the best fit, academically and financially. You can find your local advising center here – http://www.educationusa.info/centers.

Searching for financial aid will add considerable time to the overall college application process so make sure you start early. Be realistic about how much time you can give to this if you are still in high school and studying for exams.

★ ★ ★ ★ ★ ☆ ☆ ☆ ☆ ☆ ☆ ☆

Chapter Five
The College Application Process (a.k.a. College Apps)

This chapter covers the basic requirements and steps in the US college application process, and points you to some excellent web sites for international students. (Financial aid for international students is covered in *Chapter Four – Funding your College Degree*.) You won't be able to apply for a student visa unless you have committed to an offer from an American university, so don't get too distracted by the visa process at this point.

> ✔ **TIP**
>
> Some colleges will ask for passport information and as you will need it to apply for a student visa, now is an excellent time to renew or apply for a passport if you don't have a current one. A current passport must be valid for at least six months from the date you arrive in the USA. You may not be able to renew your passport if it has more than six months remaining on it, but there are embassies and consulates around the USA where you will be able to renew it as needed.

Background information

There is no overarching body, such as UCAS in the UK, through which US college applications are processed. There are Common and Universal application systems, but not all colleges use them and each college will require their own additional information:

★ **First steps**. Whether you're doing this on your own or have help from a third party, you must first visit the web site of every college you're interested in, as admission requirements differ widely and the application process begins there. As well as containing excellent and comprehensive information on their web sites, most college Admissions offices are well staffed and can answer any e-mail or phone query you have. Make the effort to forge a special relationship with the individual Admissions director/ counselor either in your country or responsible for your area.

> ⚠️ **WARNING**
> When searching for colleges make sure you're looking at the right web site as colleges often have similar-sounding names. The University of Michigan isn't the same as Michigan State, and Miami University is actually situated in Ohio.

★ **Financial aid**. If you are looking for any kind of financial aid you should include this criterion into your college considerations from day one. Although there may be funding from a third party organization, it helps to know which colleges might give you financial aid and which definitely will not. (See *Chapter Four – Funding your College Degree*.)

★ **Length of application process**. Professionals in this area advise allowing at least a year to apply to an American college as a foreign student. Not only does the application process take months and months, if you're successful, you then have to apply for the relevant visa and make travel plans.

★ **When to begin your college search**. Most American students begin their college search midway through their junior year of high school (Year 12 in the UK, or second to last year), although applications typically aren't submitted until the senior (final) year. As a foreign student, with different academic qualifications, you may have to wait until you have your results to receive an offer of a place from an American college. Some colleges will accept predicted grades but you'll need to visit individual college web sites to find this information and call their Admissions office if it's not clearly stated.

★ **When to contact a college with questions**. Although a large percentage of US colleges have strict application deadlines, the departments are fully staffed all year. This means they can take questions from you and direct you to information at any time. They are also somewhat flexible when dealing with international schools unfamiliar with the US application process.

Matthew Beatty, Director of International Admissions at Indiana University, advises, "Applicants should stay engaged with the colleges they're applying to." Although he cautions, "There is a fine line between phoning with every question when you could find the answer on the college web site." In general US college administrators are very accessible and accommodating:

★ **Demonstrated interest**. More and more colleges are looking for a *demonstrated interest* from applicants. This means you have contacted them more than once, perhaps visited the campus or met with a representative in your own country. Simply picking a college from a list of possibilities and sending in your application may put you behind applicants who have shown a continued interest in the college and have convinced that college they are keen to attend.

Colleges are looking for applicants who will accept an offer if one is made.

★ **Number of applications**. American students typically apply to five or more colleges. In this mix there will be one or two *reaches* and at least one *safety* choice. This means at least one college (the *safety*) is deemed well within your academic profile in terms of grades and scores, while the *reaches* mean you'll have to work really hard, and have great grades and test scores. In addition to this *reach* colleges typically only admit a small number of their applicants, all of whom fall into the high averages, sometimes making it a numbers game. Most of the top universities in the USA are considered *reaches* by any standard and they are extremely competitive. Think hard about your *safety* choice – if you would never consider going at all why bother applying? Find a *safety* choice you feel you could attend.

 WARNING
If you are attending, or have already attended, higher education (above high school level) you must apply as a *transfer student* rather than a freshman.

★ **Choosing colleges**. As listed in previous chapters there are web sites that allow you to narrow down your choices by various criteria, such as academic excellence, location, subject strength, and so on. There are thousands of colleges in the USA and searching via one of these web sites makes the college app process easier and less overwhelming.

★ **Schools within the college**. Some colleges have 'schools' for various subject areas such as Business, Journalism, Engineering and so on, and students may have to apply to both the college and the school if they want to major in that field. With other colleges you may not be admitted into the relevant school until you have fulfilled all your General Education requirements. (See *Chapter Two – An Overview of US Colleges* for more information on majors and minors.)

If you know your intended major it may be possible to apply to the specific school when submitting your regular college application. In many instances you will be required to complete core classes or General Education classes before taking classes for your major, and it might be a year or two before you attend classes within a specific school or department. Securing a place in a school/ department when you are accepted by the college will avoid a gamble later. The gamble is although the college may accept you, if you aren't accepted into your desired school at the same time you will have to apply after your first or second year, and you are not automatically guaranteed a place. Getting straight into your school of choice allows you to start taking classes that are pre-requisites for your major.

If you don't apply to a specific school or don't know your intended major, there's no problem at all – you will simply be accepted into the general undergraduate program to take your required core classes.

★ **Honors programs and colleges**. Many colleges have honors programs and some larger universities now have honors colleges under their umbrellas. There are also national honor societies with a presence in many colleges, such as the nation's oldest, Phi Beta Kappa (pronounced Fie Bayta Kappa). Honor societies recognize students with the highest academic scores and grades. Some students with high scores are automatically accepted onto an honors program and need only notify the college if they want to decline this offer. Other colleges require a supplemental application for consideration by the honors program/ college. Requirements at application and throughout the four-year degree course differ from one institution to another. National Honor

Societies are often by invitation only. If you don't make it onto the honors program it doesn't necessarily mean you won't get into the college – most colleges consider applicants for general admission first and then look again when deciding on honors placement.

The stated benefits of being an honors student include smaller classes, special activities and events, scholarship opportunities, an honors degree on graduation and, of course, a potentially more dazzling résumé (CV). You are often allowed to register for classes earlier as an honors student. It is generally agreed that honors programs present a more rigorous academic challenge to students.

 TIP

More and more colleges are now offering honors housing, where academically stellar students can live in the same buildings. Typically this housing is extremely competitive and applicants either have to test in, or submit high test scores and high school grades.

★ **Special interest groups**. Many colleges now offer special interest affiliation housing. As explained in *Chapter Eight – Before You Go – Visa Application and Other Important Steps*, this allows lower classmen to mingle with students of like interests at a time when they may not yet be taking classes in those particular subjects. At some colleges this application is part of the general housing application (which comes once you have accepted a place at college), but some colleges may require you to either test in on your chosen subject area, or submit slightly higher than average test scores or school grades. Again, should you fail to obtain the special interest placement it won't necessarily mean you fail to get into the college itself.

How to apply

When filling out application forms/ materials **always use your name as it appears on your passport**. Everything you need to know about how to apply to a specific college is on its web site, including an online application form. In most cases you will need to set up an account to register – although this doesn't imply a commitment – and you can still make enquiries without registering. Although there is an application fee it isn't required until you hit the 'Send' button and submit an application – setting up an account doesn't usually create a financial commitment.

 TIP

Creating an account will help show *demonstrated interest* if needed and will ensure you receive updates and newsletters from that college.

Types of applications

Although some colleges look primarily at your academic information, US colleges in general take a much more holistic approach to recruiting than you are probably used to. The application forms will ask what, besides your grades and test results, you can bring to their campus. It is important to appreciate this approach when completing your application forms.

There are three basic types of application and each college will specify which one(s) it requires:

★ Individual Application
★ The Common Application (App)
★ The Universal Application

Individual Application

The college has its own application form on the web site that you may either complete and submit online, or send in as a printed document. College applications are similar but not the same, so you should read the guidelines and the form carefully. Some colleges will give you a choice between using their own application form or the Common/ Universal App (see below). Many experts advise submitting the college's own application form as it allows you to give more tailored information, but using the Common App might speed things up a little.

 WARNING

If you are completing a handful of individual apps that are very similar make sure you don't submit identical personal essays. Although your essay theme may be the same, college admissions personnel often know each other (through high school visits and college fairs) and your self-plagiarizing might come to light, particularly if it's a gripping personal story.

The Common App

The Common App is a standardized first-year application form used by more than 400 colleges in the US. Specific college web sites will tell you immediately if they require you to submit an application through the Common App web site. A few give you the choice between individual and Common App and guarantee no preference is given to either. The Common App web site gives a list of participating colleges, together with their deadlines, fees and requirements – www.commonapp.org. As many popular colleges now use the Common App, it is an excellent way of viewing a lot of information on one site:

★ Information included on each member college includes:
- Type of admissions process
- Application fee
- Supplements needed on application
- Standardized tests and scores needed (ACT, SAT, Language proficiency)

★ If using the Common App, member colleges are required to look at the whole student not only their academic records. If your grades and test scores are weaker than your other strengths a Common App college would take everything into consideration. According to the Common App web site : '*Membership is limited to colleges and universities that evaluate students using a holistic selection process. A holistic process includes subjective as well as objective criteria, including at least one recommendation form, at least one untimed essay, and broader campus diversity considerations*'.

★ Although the Common App simplifies the application process, most colleges require supplemental information from all applicants and more from international applicants. Unfortunately, the extra information you will be asked for will not be the same from every college. Don't overlook this section in the Common App process or your application will be considered *incomplete*.

★ You are allowed to submit additional materials with your Common App, but if you are unsure whether this is necessary, think carefully about what that additional material might accomplish or call the college Admissions office for guidance.

★ Supplements can be submitted with your Common App (such as information about Art or Athletics) if you wish to have a specific talent considered, or if you are trying for athletic recruitment. Not all colleges accept this information so it might not always be available. Supplement deadlines differ from one college to another.

★ The Common App asks questions about possible areas of academic concentration and possible professional plans. If you're like the majority of applicants and don't really know, it is okay to leave these sections blank.

★ If your high school does not have a dedicated college counselor as many American high schools do, your principal or head teacher can complete and submit the school information instead. The term *college counselor* is the equivalent of a careers officer in some schools. The web site allows you to identify a school staff member, and an e-mail is sent to that person with log in information. You can then keep track of what your teachers are submitting. Rena Nathanson, an American living in London, has recently gone through the Common App process with her son who was born and educated in England. She advises both students and parents, "Try to find an advocate at your school."

★ The Common App web site contains a great deal of help and FAQs for international students.

★ The web site contains separate help guidelines for applicants and for school officials.

★ If you can't find the answer to any question in the FAQs, go to the 'Contact' tab, and type in a key word for your question. This will bring up many answers and may produce the one you're looking for. If this fails contact the support team directly and send your specific question. In my experience answers are sent very quickly and are accurate. There is no published telephone number.

★ There is no fee for using the Common App other than the original college application fee.

WARNING

Rena Nathanson also advises, "Keep checking your Common App account as the information about required supplemental information comes in almost on a daily basis. Even when it says your applications are complete, keep checking, because next day it could tell you that you need to submit something else. In addition, the information has to come from the school and not the student or parent."

Universal College Application

The Universal App is a less widely used application form that also sends your application information to several colleges at the same time. Its member colleges are listed on the home page. The difference between this and the Common App is that member colleges may use the information as they see fit and are not required to look holistically at applicants – www.universalcollegeapp.com.

 TIP

Although completing and submitting applications is a demanding and lengthy process, if you are really stuck and can't find your answer from the relevant web site, phone your college of interest directly and speak to someone in the Admissions office or International Students Office. They are very likely to know the answer to your question.

Rolling admissions

A *rolling admissions* process means colleges are taking applications on a continuous basis (within a fairly wide window) rather than having specific deadlines. While this can make for a less stressful college application, you should bear a few things in mind:

★ Spots are filled as desirable candidates apply, so it's more of a 'first come, first served' system. Applicants are generally advised to apply at the start rather than at the end of the window.

★ As spots are filled this may mean financial aid and housing are allocated at the same time.

★ Even if you are comfortable applying later, if you are seeking financial aid from the college there may be an earlier deadline to apply for that.

★ Colleges with rolling admissions may require you to accept or decline their offer before you have heard from your other colleges. Ask when you are required to accept/ decline an offer before you submit your application. You may also be required to apply for housing to secure your place.

★ CRDA (Candidates' Reply Date Agreement) and NCRD (National Candidates' Reply Date) – many colleges (including those with rolling admissions) subscribe to the CRDA, or are members of NACAC (National Association for College Admission Counseling), and must allow you till May 1 to reply to their offers and send in your tuition deposit. If you feel you must accept an offer before you have heard back from other colleges, you will generally only lose your deposit if you change your mind.

Waiting till May 1 to let a college know your answer doesn't jeopardize anything as the college has already made you an offer. (See *Chapter 7 – Offers and Rejections* for more information on accepting and declining offers.)

Deadlines

If you are applying to a handful of colleges keep track of the deadlines as they can be anywhere from November to the following

March. Although many colleges have similar deadlines, they're not all at the same time. Pay attention to all deadlines and work on the earlier applications first:

★ Some colleges have different application deadlines for international students so make sure you have searched specifically for this information.

★ If you are applying for a place on an honors program, there may be an earlier deadline.

★ The Petersons web site has a list of colleges with late admissions deadlines – http://www.petersons.com/college-search/late-deadline-schools.aspx.

★ DO NOT miss the application deadline posted on the web site as this could jeopardize your chances of success. Having said that, as an international applicant, you may have extenuating circumstances which may cause you to miss a deadline. Always let the college know if this is the case and don't assume you've 'blown it' – many colleges are flexible in such situations.

★ DO NOT omit any part of the application packet you are required to complete otherwise your application will be considered *incomplete* – in other words, no one will be looking at it until all the required information is included. Furthermore, the admissions department may not notify you that your application is incomplete.

★ Keep track of your application online if you can and make sure all components, such as test scores and letters of recommendation, are received by the Admissions office.

★ If you are applying for any type of financial aid make sure you do not miss this deadline. Colleges look at thousands of applications and if yours isn't in on time the money may be allocated elsewhere.

Early Decision and Early Action

Many colleges allow applicants to apply either ED (Early Decision) or EA (Early Action). If there is a college you would definitely attend were you offered a place, this is an attractive option:

★ **Early Decision** has an earlier application deadline and makes offers earlier than the regular admissions process (usually December). Always check individual college web sites for deadline information as this can change regularly. You can only apply ED to one college and if you are accepted, you must take up the place at that college. You may submit regular apps to other colleges, but these must be withdrawn if your ED application is successful. Colleges honor one another's ED systems and will not offer a place if you have an ED offer elsewhere. Not all colleges offer ED so check the web site.

Many colleges make a high percentage of offers to ED students, so if you are sure about your college choice it's an easy gamble to take. Call the college if it's not clear on the web site how many ED applicants are successful and remember to make sure you can compete with the caliber of successful applicants. If you are wavering about where you want to attend ED is probably not for you.

Some colleges offer a second round of ED applications with a January deadline. Again, you are only allowed one ED application and it is binding.

You are advised to submit regular applications to other colleges of interest even if you are applying ED to one college. This will ensure you have other options to fall back on should your ED application be unsuccessful.

★ **Early Action** applications also have an earlier deadline and notification, but are not binding on the student. Single Choice Early Action (SCEA) means you can only apply early to one college using the EA process although it is still non-binding. The benefit to students is they hear back from colleges earlier than with regular applications, so if you're worried about time constraints this may be an option for you.

★ **REA** is Restricted Early Action. A handful of colleges now have REA, whereby, for example, you may not apply ED or EA to any other college.

⚠ **WARNING**

If you decide to apply early this will affect the deadline for taking standardized tests such as ACT or SAT, as colleges will require your scores earlier than regular applicants. It will also affect any financial aid you apply for as most colleges allocate aid during regular application time. (See *Chapter Four – Funding your College Degree* for financial aid information, and *Chapter Six – Standardized Tests (ACT and SAT)*, for ACT and SAT details.) Check individual admissions pages for this crucial information.

★ In all the above cases you may be *deferred*. While this is a pain it isn't the end of the world – it simply means you are put into the general pool of *regular* applicants and will receive a decision at the same time as everyone else. If you are *rejected*, as opposed to *deferred*, this means you are no longer being considered in any applicant pool. (See *Chapter Seven – Offers and Rejections* for details on acceptances and rejections.)

★ Some colleges do not offer ED or EA, preferring only to admit or deny applicants.

How to complete the Admissions packet

Most college web sites are easy to follow with regard to admissions. There is usually a tab on the home page for 'Admissions', and either an 'International students' or 'Freshmen/ Undergraduate Applications' tab. Unless your high school follows the US system, skip all information regarding academic credit/ hours requirements as this will only confuse matters. There should be specific information for international academic requirements. Once you get to the correct page, bookmark it. College web sites vary so much you might not remember how to return to specific pages in the future. Once on the desired page there will probably be an applications checklist, which I strongly recommend you print out and keep in a binder or folder:

★ As mentioned in the first chapter, college admission requirements differ around the country. Some colleges only look at academic scores, but most take a more holistic approach looking at everything from your schoolwork to your sporting interests and what you do in your spare time. Extra-curricular* activities are huge in the States, and many college applicants will have spent the previous four years (sometimes longer) building up their résumés. If your résumé is weak concentrate on colleges looking primarily at academics, and if you're not a top rate academic, look for colleges that take other factors into consideration. (This information is on the web sites.) Belonging to one club, or having only one hobby, may not be a match for the kids who've been class president, editor of the school newspaper, captain of a sports team or ranked top of their class academically. The competition is fierce.

---

* Extra-curricular activities is the term used for activities outside of school. Hobbies, interests, internships and work are all relevant, and help show you as a well-rounded person. Express your passion and commitment to a few activities rather than a passing interest in a dozen. Colleges are looking for quality versus quantity.

According to Peterson's (College Bound) web site: '*Colleges aren't terribly picky about how you spend your down time, as long as you're doing something meaningful. They won't know if you spend hours upon hours playing video games; they will certainly notice a lack of notable activities on your college application.*' Visit the web site for more information on what colleges are looking for – http://www.petersons.com/college-search/extracurricular-involvement-college-acceptance.aspx.

Colleges are looking for proof you are a good fit for them and you will contribute to their campus and thrive there. The University of California, Los Angeles (UCLA) explains its admissions policy very well on its web site. UCLA looks for applicants: '*...who would contribute the most to UCLA's dynamic learning environment; they are also the applicants who would make the most of being immersed in it. Although high school grade point average and standardized test scores are important indicators of academic achievement used in UCLA's admissions review, they only tell part of the story*'. If you are applying to a college that requires non-academic information, I would advise reading the UCLA page if your college's own page isn't very explanatory – http://www.admissions.ucla.edu/Prospect/Adm_fr/FrSel.htm

★ According to the National Association for College Admission Counseling (NACAC), small colleges generally take a more 'holistic' approach, while larger colleges are more 'mechanical' in their application review process, looking more at test scores and high school academic credentials. Because of the wide variety in home school education, colleges usually rely on test scores (i.e. ACT/ SAT) in applications from home-schooled students.

What you'll need to submit your application

1. Completed application form
2. GPA (Grade Point Average) equivalent/ academic records

(transcripts), possibly sent via a third party organization
3. Standardized test scores – SAT/ ACT scores (in most cases) sent direct from the testing body to the college, see *Chapter Six – Standardized Tests (ACT and SAT)* for comprehensive information on these tests
4. Official translations if records are not in English
5. Proof of English Proficiency test scores (if English isn't your first language)
6. Certificate of Finances for International Students (CFIS)
7. Class ranking (if applicable)
8. Letters of recommendation
9. Personal essays, in many cases
10. Passport details, in many cases

1. Completed application form

If using the Common App or the Universal College Application, the college web site will direct you to that web site. Otherwise, the college's own application form will be on the web site for you to complete. International students may be asked to complete the 'International School Supplement' portion of the Common App, which allows college admissions staff to better understand your academic records and qualifications:

★ Please note, when stating your type of school, a *public* school in the USA is a state school and not a private or independent school. Your *counselor* refers to the member of your school staff who is advising you about college and career paths.

★ When supplying the information for each of the four years of high school, 12th grade refers to your final year, 11th grade to your second last year and so on. (Year 12 and 13 in the UK.)

2. GPA equivalent/ academic records (transcripts)

American colleges look closely at an applicant's high school GPA (Grade Point Average), which foreign students usually don't have.

A GPA is the record of a high school student's grade average throughout high school or throughout the final two years. There is no official grade conversion between the US grading system and other education systems, so if you don't have a GPA leave this blank and don't attempt to figure it out for yourself:

TIP

If you are applying to play an NCAA sport at D1 or D2 level, the NCAA has its own method of converting international high school information into a GPA equivalent – http://www.ncaapublications.com/productdownloads/IS10.pdf.

★ No matter where you studied at high/ secondary school, an American college will require your academic records, referred to as *transcripts* (if available), and certified translations if the originals are not in English. If you attended more than one high/ secondary school you must provide records from each of them.

★ Some colleges are able to vet foreign academic credentials themselves, while others require you to have them 'evaluated' by an independent organization. If you have specific colleges in mind, ask the Admissions staff whether or not you need to obtain *credential evaluation services*. These are not free and you will need to allow extra time for this paperwork to be processed. Don't employ a company until you are sure the report is required and the college will accept it.

The US government does not technically require credential evaluation companies for visa purposes. However, many colleges require applicants to use them and as they issue the I-20 (which you need for a visa application), you may not have a choice. If you are not told which company to use it is generally recommended you use a member of the National Association of Credential

Evaluation Services – http://www.naces.org or the AACRAO's International Education Services – http://ies.aacrao.org. Always check with your college before beginning this process, as refunds may be hard to obtain.

★ It is most important that when you are told to obtain your academic credentials from 'the institution' where you sat them (or words to that effect) this means from **the relevant examinations board** and not from your high school. If you don't know which examining body you used, ask your high school. The academic credentials must be sent directly from the examining board to the evaluation company and sometimes e-mails are not acceptable.

Make sure that if you use an evaluation company it is doing what your college requests. Steve, a British high school student, was required to use a well-established credential evaluation service when applying to his desired US college. The company failed to have examination results sent from the correct body, but despite this Steve was somehow still able to attend. Unfortunately, the error was discovered later and his credentials were still an issue at the end of the spring semester, meaning he could not register for the following year until the matter was resolved.

✔ **TIP**

If you can avoid using one of these companies it will save you time and money, so check with your prospective college as soon as you can. Depending on the country you are coming from, your examining board may be able to send your credentials directly to the colleges you specify, thus cutting out the middleman. If the college has a regional representative in your country, s/ he may be able to give you information on this.

★ A handful of American colleges are members of the International Association of Universities. This association has members from many countries, its aim being to promote the 'internationalization' of higher education. If you are having problems with your academic credentials, and the American college in question is an IAU member, it might be worth seeking assistance from the regional representative. Check the web site for further details – www.iau-aiu.net.

★ Fulbright has a sample transcript for UK schools which shows British applicants how to submit a transcript to a US college. The same web page has blank transcripts for completion and extensive guidelines for submitting academic information – http://www.fulbright.org.uk/study-in-the-usa/undergraduate-study/applying/transcript.

📖 **FURTHER READING**
Visit the Fulbright web site for your specific country to find detailed and comprehensive college application help. This information is valuable whether or not you are applying to the Fulbright program.

3. Standardized tests ACT/ SAT

Please refer to *Chapter Six – Standardized Tests (ACT and SAT)* for all information on these tests.

4. Official translations

If your high school records are not in English you will be required to have a certified third party provide an official translation. Most colleges either name specific companies you must use, or give you a few to choose from. This is not free although some companies can give you a price quote very quickly based on the word count of the documents in question. Automated translation software, which allows you to translate your own documents, is not usually accepted nor is it 100% accurate. If your college does not name a specific company, look for one that is a member of either the National Association of Credential Evaluation Services (NACES) or the Association of International Credential Services (AICE). You may be required to send the original documents once a college accepts you, but don't send them unless specifically asked.

5. Proof of English Proficiency test scores

If English isn't your first language, scores from a language proficiency test are usually required – the most widely used are:

★ TOEFL (Test of English as a Foreign Language) – www.toeflgoanywhere.org.

★ IELTS (International English Language Testing System) – www.IELTS.org.

★ PTE (Pearson Test of English) – www.pearsonpte.com.

The language proficiency requirement may be waived for applicants with a high score on the SAT Critical Reading section, and some colleges post a list of exempt countries too. Check specific college web sites for test preferences and score minimum requirements and don't assume all colleges are the same in this matter. The scores must be sent directly from the testing body.

All three of the above-mentioned test companies offer the following:

★ Their web sites contain a list of US colleges that accept their scores.

★ The tests measure how well you read, listen, speak and write in English and are administered at hundreds, if not thousands of test sites around the globe.

★ There are practice materials on the web sites.

★ Tests are typically taken online, although there are some exceptions. They are administered several times per month, with dates and registration options available at the web sites.

★ The fee depends on where you live and there are additional fees for late registration and for changing your test date.

★ Registration opens up about three to four months before each test and you should register early to get the date you want.

★ You can have your test scores sent to several colleges, although the processes differ with each company. With all three, having your test scores automatically sent to colleges is optional.

★ You can usually take the test as many times as you wish.

★ Score requirements (i.e. desired test results) are specified by individual colleges rather than by the testing body, so check on college web sites. If you are applying to a specific school or department within a college, check their page on the web site in case they have different score requirements.

★ Your scores are posted online between five days and two weeks after the test. (IELTS sends some scores through regular mail.)

★ The results are valid for two years, after which time they cannot be reported to colleges.

Some colleges will offer conditional admission if your English proficiency test scores do not meet their requirements. The college will usually require you to attend an English language class of their choosing, often called a Pathway or Foundation program. Once you have successfully completed the program you will be admitted to the regular undergraduate degree program. You can also re-take and submit standardized language tests such as TOEFL before such a class would begin.

📖 FURTHER READING
According to the Inside Higher Ed web site: '*The pathway approach, in which students enroll in a mix of academic and credit-bearing English coursework in a foundation semester or year, continues to grow in popularity. The programs appeal to international students who wish to begin academic coursework right away, for financial or other reasons*' – http://www.insidehighered.com/news/2013/01/03/conditional-admission-and-pathway-programs-proliferate

6. Certificate of Finances for International Students (CFIS)

Colleges are required by the US government to ask for this certificate. Without proof of funds to cover your first year of expenses (tuition, room and board) at the college to which you're applying, that college cannot issue a certificate of eligibility, (usually Form I-20) which you'll need to apply for a student visa. If you have already been offered scholarship funds from this university or an outside body (e.g. an athletic scholarship) this amount counts toward the required amount and is included on the form. Some colleges also accept student loan approvals on this form.

Colleges will either have their own customized form to complete or they will attach the College Board's International Student Certificate of Finances Guidelines, with examples of the form.

Many colleges have a payment plan whereby your parents (or sponsors) do not have to empty their bank account before you get to college. Such payment plans typically ask for about 40% of your first year tuition, room and board up front, and then there are three-monthly payment deadlines throughout the year.

 WARNING
You will be required to specify the type of visa you require when filling out the CFIS form, so make sure you know which visa you need. Most undergraduates apply for an F1 visa.

7. Class ranking
Some colleges will ask for your *class ranking*, which is the percentage or quartile value US high schools use to measure students against each other. If your high school doesn't rank (and many don't) this does not negatively affect an application and you should simply state that your high school does not rank.

8. Letters of recommendation
Colleges often ask for two or three letters of recommendation from your high school – usually one must be from a teacher, while the others can be from college/ careers counselors or another teacher. You are generally allowed to choose the letter writers but make sure to ask their permission before submitting their names. Think carefully about the teacher(s) who write these letters. Colleges want to find out about you as an individual, as well as an academic student. Select a teacher you feel knows you well.

Remember your teachers are very busy and their letters may take some time to get to the colleges in question. You may be asked if you wish to waive the right to see your teacher letters – your high school may even have a policy about this.

✔ **TIP**

For high school teachers. Don't understate your students' achievements, ability and potential when writing references or recommendations. Colleges are interested in academic ability, but also want to know about student participation, commitment, learning style and so on. Anything positive you can say about the individual is welcomed.

To the horror of some applicants, colleges may also ask for a letter of recommendation from parents, classmates or a sibling. Resist your urge to assume this is a joke – if they suggest such a letter, it will be taken seriously if submitted. They are usually optional and colleges would not penalize if such a letter were not included. If you receive this request, talk to your parents/ friends about it, even if it goes against everything in your culture or personality. And if your parents aren't the gushing type, it's probably best to omit the letter.

9. Personal essays

Most applications will ask for one or two essays of a personal nature. Typical questions are:

★ Describe a setback you have encountered in your life. Explain how you have handled the situation and what you have learned from it.

★ Tell us anything else you want us to know about yourself that you haven't had the opportunity to write about elsewhere in the application.

★ Discuss some issue of personal, local, national, or international concern and its importance to you.

★ Indicate a person who has had a significant influence on you, and describe their influence.

★ International students may be asked to discuss what they hope to take back to their home country after studying in the USA, and other questions regarding culture.

This is your chance to show your chosen colleges who you really are and why they should offer you a place. It is also your opportunity to include information about yourself not communicated in any other part of the application.

The Penn Group hosts a great web site that covers everything on college application essays, with examples of what to do and what to avoid – www.college-admission-essay.com. Because of the risk of plagiarism personal essays are highly scrutinized, and admissions professionals can usually tell when an applicant hasn't written his or her own essay.

Stick to the designated word limit and think carefully about how much you can communicate within that limit. The Common App has a word limit of 500, which you should adhere to. Individual colleges reading your application (sent through the Common App) differ in their approach to essays longer than 500 words. Some colleges, such as Harvard and Pepperdine, strongly urge applicants to follow the guidelines closely, while others, such as Bucknell, are lenient on the limit. In general, colleges prefer applicants to be concise – http://www.collegemapper.com/blog/2012/08/the-common-app-500-word-limit-21-more-colleges-weigh-in/.

✔ **TIP**

Write about something meaningful to you and write in a genuine manner. Don't try to guess what the college wants to hear – they want to hear *your* 'voice'. Make sure you build in enough time to draft and polish these essays. For many students it takes a few weeks before the essay is ready for submission.

10. Passport details

Check specific web sites as many colleges ask for your passport details and/ or a photocopy to be sent with your application. Most countries have *busy times* for passport applications (e.g. before the summer), when the processing time can double or triple. Make sure you build in enough time to obtain or renew a passport if needed. Your passport should be valid for at least six months when you first enter the USA as a student.

General guidelines for applying to college

Although college web sites don't always state the following points specifically, it is generally advised to pay attention to them:

★ **Use your official name**. When you apply to colleges either through the Common App web site or through the individual site, you will usually be required to set up an account. **Always use your name as it appears on official documents such as your passport**. This is extremely important – your college offer letter might be required as part of your visa application, therefore it must match your official documentation. If you use anything other than your official name with colleges, this name will appear on the I-20 paperwork generated by the college and it won't match your passport.

★ **Get organized**. Parent Rena Nathan remembers her son's application process was, "… very stressful. There's a lot of information going out and coming back at you; students should find someone to help them." As you will probably be applying to more than one college get yourself organized from the start – bookmark all web pages relevant to your account information, and make a list of log in information and passwords. As you progress through the application process, particularly if you're successful, you may find yourself with more than one account for the same college (e.g. accepted students, housing, class registration), and it can get very confusing. More importantly, not being able to find or remember your password may result in having to have it re-sent while crucial deadlines come and go.

★ **Complete the application yourself**. Especially any essays or personal statements. College admissions professionals can tell immediately if a parent or consultant has been over-involved in an application and some colleges have a policy not to work with education consultants or other agents. Write from the heart rather than trying to anticipate what the Admissions people want to read. There are many web sites with examples of great essays, tips for writing your own, and 'what to avoid' pointers, which you should definitely read if you're not sure what to write.

★ **Avoid plagiarism**. American colleges are very tough on plagiarism and college applications are now on the radar too. Companies such as Turnitin – http://turnitin.com/ produce software allowing Admissions staff to submit all applicant-generated documents to a vast database of Internet content, subscription content, and previously submitted documents. A report is produced highlighting matches in application documents. In short, if you use anyone else's material you should credit or cite your source as you would in any academic paper. If you are asked for original material by one college, don't repackage something you've written before as it could be out there in the Ethernet – www.plagiarism.org has FAQs about plagiarism of every kind.

★ **Checking the application packet**. When you have completed your application packet, ask someone else to look it over. This includes your personal essays. If you've written about your home life or upbringing and don't want your parents to read it, have a friend or teacher check it. Be careful not to over-edit, as colleges want to hear your voice. Never submit a college application riddled with spelling and grammar errors, especially if you are applying to Journalism and other writing-based schools or departments. Admissions departments do not look kindly on sloppy applications and some reviewers make their first cut based solely on typos and spelling errors.

★ **Make copies**. Print out or make copies of everything you send off in applications to all colleges, particularly if you are asked to send original documents such as transcripts and financial information. You may need them for your visa application and for entering the USA.

★ **Tracking your application**. Many college web sites allow you to track the process of your application online. Find out whether this is available and if so, check to see when every piece of your application is received into the system, especially information coming from a third party such as teachers, and translation services. While actual decisions are not usually given over the phone, the staff member might be able to tell you if part of your application (i.e. a letter of recommendation) hasn't arrived. It's up to you to nudge a tardy reference writer if a letter of recommendation hasn't shown up. If you're applying to more than one college, the timing of when you hear back from your colleges can be crucial.

★ **Offers and Rejections**. Many colleges now send offers and rejections via e-mail, so once they have all your information keep checking back for the decision. (See *Chapter Seven – Offers and Rejections* for information on how to respond to offers and rejections.)

Student athlete applications

Sports play a huge part in college life in the USA both for players and fans. There are a wide variety of sports played at top competition levels or played just for fun. According to the NCAA (National Collegiate Athletics Association), the number of international athletes at US colleges has increased by more than 1,000% in the last ten years.

Intercollegiate sports

Most colleges in the USA have many sports teams representing them in competition against other colleges. College sports in the USA is big business and extremely competitive. If you are interested in playing a sport at a US college you not only have to beat out most of the competition, but your grades and test scores must still meet minimum requirements. Most student athletes are not scouted by coaches – it's up to you as an applicant to attract the attention of coaches and get yourself an offer. This is in part because coaches are strictly regulated as to when they can contact potential applicants.

In many sports, students can usually play at one of three levels for their college – Division I (called DI), Division 2 (DII) and Division 3 (DIII). DI is the top tier and requires talent, plus hours and hours of practice and play. Some students opt for DII and even DIII to ensure they can play and keep up with the academic demands, but D3 sports programs don't offer scholarships and neither do the IVY League colleges and universities. (See *Chapter Four – Funding your College Degree* for information on financial aid):

★ To play a college sport at *varsity* level, you must still meet minimum academic requirements and submit a regular application to the Admissions office. In most cases the coach pertaining to your sport will also be involved in this process. As well as thinking about your ability as a student athlete, you should also be looking at how you stack up academically against the regular applicant pool of high school students.

★ Before taking any steps, such as signing up with a search agency, familiarize yourself with the entire college sports scene. You should research what is required of international students and the international student web site has a good general overview of this – http://blog.internationalstudent.com/2010/06/international-student-athletes-in-the-usa/.

★ Visit the National Collegiate Athletic Association (NCAA) web site for a comprehensive overview and information on recruitment – www.ncaa.org. The NCAA is the main governing body of college sports and has many rules and regulations relating to students, coaches and colleges. The introductory videos are your first point of entry on this site – http://web1.ncaa.org/ECWR2/NCAA_EMS/NCAA.jsp. There is specific information for international students under the 'Resources' tab, including the credentials required by country of origin.

★ The National Association of Intercollegiate Athletes has about 350 member colleges and 60,000 student athletes – www.naia.org. It too has specific information for international applicants, and eligibility requirements, which you can find here – http://www.playnaia.org/page/international.php.

★ For students attending two-year Junior or Community colleges, the governing body is the NJCAA (National Junior College Athletic Association) – www.njcaa.org.

★ All three bodies have strict eligibility requirements you must fulfill before being considered as a student athlete with them. Most applicants will be completing a sizable athletics application, usually after the regular college application, so you should factor extra time if this is your dream.

> **⚠ WARNING**
> If you have been playing at professional club level in your country, this may affect your amateur status according to NCAA rules. Likewise if you received a stipend this could be classed as payment if the amount exceeded expenses reimbursement.

Your first step is to find out where you can play your sport at an intercollegiate level. By looking at the web sites of the NCAA, the NAIA and the NJCAA you can find the sports they govern and the member colleges:

★ **The NCAA** covers 23 sports, and you can perform searches by sport, state or division at this page – http://www.ncaa.org/wps/wcm/ connect/public/ncaa/about+the+ncaa/who+we+are+landing+page.

The NCAA states: '*Any college-bound student-athlete (incoming freshman or first-year enrollee) interested in enrolling at an NCAA Division I or II college or university and competing as a varsity student-athlete on behalf of that NCAA school's intercollegiate athletics program, must receive an academic and amateurism evaluation certification decision from the NCAA Eligibility Center.*'

This eligibility application requires the same documentation as for a regular college application, that is, official high school transcripts, certified copies of certificates, official translations of records (if necessary) ACT/ SAT scores and so on. Full instructions are available at the NCAA web site – http://www.ncaapublications.com/productdownloads/IS10.pdf. To register with the NCAA, go to www.eligibilitycenter.org.

Division III sports do not have NCAA eligibility rules and you are advised to work with the coach at your colleges of interest regarding admission as a student athlete.

★ **The NAIA** web site states that its sports are Basketball (D1 and D2), Baseball, Bowling, Cheer and Dance, Cross Country, (American) Football, Golf, Indoor Track and Field, Outdoor Track and Field, Softball, Tennis, Volleyball and Wrestling. Even if you are certified with the NCAA, if you want to play in the NAIA you must receive certification from that body. It also has specific application guidelines for international students – http://www.playnaia.org/d/international/NAIA_GuideforInternationalStudents.pdf.

★ **The NJCAA** has its list of sports here – http://www.njcaa.org/sports.cfm. You can select a college by region, sport or state. It also has rules and requirements regarding eligibility.

Most colleges suggest you make direct contact with the relevant coach at your college of interest. Before doing so you should compile a sports résumé (CV) detailing your experience, scores, awards and so on, together with a letter of recommendation from your current coach. This should be e-mailed with a letter of introduction and you should ask the coach if other information, such as a performance movie clip, is required. Many college web sites now contain an athletic survey, which you should complete and submit if required.

Finding a coach's contact information can be done in several ways. If you already have colleges in mind, go to the web sites and follow the links for Athletics or Sports. It may take some time to find the contact information because most college sports web sites also contain information about the current sport season, future games and ticket sales. Somewhere in the information will be coach names for each sport or for the Athletics department. Failing that, you should contact the Admissions office and ask where to find athletic information.

You can also find links to many college Athletics departments through the three governing bodies listed above. Alternatively, if your sport has a separate US or worldwide association, you might find college details there.

Once you have made contact and the coach has expressed interest, keep in touch with him/ her but don't become a nuisance. Whenever you are asked to forward information follow up to confirm it was received – when you send in your college application, let the coach know too. If you are an attractive athletic recruit the coaches will be in touch with the Admissions department regarding your application.

If a coach is really interested in you, s/ he may ask you to apply ED – before doing so, you should try to get some sense of whether or not this would be successful. Do not be shy about asking and remember an ED application is binding.

If you are in need of financial aid it is common to ask the coach or the Admissions office for a *pre-read* of your application for aid. In some instances the coach or the college will be able to give you an idea of the aid package it can offer.

In its brochure for international students (above) the NCAA states: '*Under no circumstances should an international student athlete be issued a Form I-20 with the expectation of financial support from the athletics office before the student has been certified as a final qualifier by the NCAA Eligibility Center or is determined to be a partial qualifier in Division II. Doing so opens the possibility for an international student who might not be eligible for financial aid to obtain a visa and enter the United States without having the sufficient funds to cover tuition and living expenses, as required by immigration laws.*'

In other words if you have been promised financial aid as part of a sports package, then you arrive at college and fail to meet NCAA eligibility requirements, your sports package will probably disappear, leaving you *out of status* because you would not have sufficient funds to cover your college expenses. The NCAA reports that some students have been sent home because of this.

As the path of your student athlete application will depend on your sport, the college and the coach, it is not possible to say with any certainty what will be required of you when applying. Although you must submit an academic application like any other student, some coaches are more heavily involved with the process.

As with all international students you must apply for, and maintain, your Non-Immigrant visa status. (See *Chapter Eight – Before You Go – Visa Application and Other Important Steps*, and *Chapter Nine – On Arrival.*)

Club sports and intramural sports

If you want to continue to play sports at college but not at the top levels, there is plenty of opportunity to play at the club or intramural level:

★ In club sports you try out for the team (as opposed to being recruited) and play against other colleges. Club sports are often just as competitive as the D1 level. At some colleges the only sports teams they have are at club level.

★ Intramural sport means you compete against other teams or individuals at your college. Although these sports programs are more for fun, they are strictly organized as far as membership and involvement are concerned. There will be a registration period and if the sport in question has multiple levels, perhaps a try-out to place you.

To find the necessary information search 'intramural sports' or 'recreational sports' on your college's web site.

Chapter Six
Standardized Tests (ACT and SAT)

These exams are not the same as British A Levels, the IB or other high school tests. Most colleges require either ACT or SAT scores as part of a college application. Every student I interviewed for this book stressed the importance of being well prepared for these tests. Because they are so different from most other high school exams, my interviewees all undertook intensive tutoring or studying before taking a test. Tanya Rehki, an Indian student on the east coast reports, "Studying and taking the SATs was the most difficult time for me. I had a hard time studying for the critical reading and writing sections because I did not grow up in an environment where English was spoken correctly. At such a late age it was difficult trying to learn the structure of a sentence and answer questions."

The ACT and SAT tests are administered by two different bodies and are not affiliated with high schools or colleges. Most colleges accept either test score, so it pays to familiarize yourself with the different styles and take the one where you feel you'd get the best results – see next section for more details:

★ Not all American colleges require ACT/ SAT scores. A few (e.g. American University in Washington DC) specifically tell international applicants NOT to send in these test scores. Others (e.g. Rollins College in Florida) allow you to waive those scores, but request additional personal information instead. If you have a particular college in mind as your top choice, it would pay to read their Admissions section thoroughly to avoid unnecessary work. If you don't know where you want to go, take one or both tests so you can submit scores anywhere.

★ The National Center for Fair and Open Testing web site contains a list of colleges where the ACT and SAT tests are optional – www.fairtest.org/university/optional. However, do make sure the test is optional for international applicants.

★ If you don't want to take the ACT or SAT because you typically don't do well in exams, consider taking one anyway. If your score is low you can either apply to colleges that don't ask for test scores, or apply to colleges looking at your other attributes too. Philip, an American high school student I know, couldn't get his ACT score above a 24 but did very well at high school – he therefore applied (successfully) to schools that didn't require the score. After multiple offers from these schools he decided to apply to colleges asking for a minimum ACT score of 28. To his surprise he was also successful with these applications. (See below for average ACT and SAT scores.)

★ High school exams are generally not a substitute for ACT/ SAT testing unless there are no testing centers in your country (see below). However, some colleges (such as Yale) allow A Level results to substitute for SAT Subject tests on a one-for-one basis. Applicants must still take either the SAT Reasoning Test or the ACT Plus Writing test. Predicted A Level scores typically cannot substitute in this way.

★ If you are applying directly to a specific school within the college, such as Engineering or Pre-Med, you may be required to take a specific SAT subject test, such as Math. The Admissions page on the college web site will give details.

★ Both the ACT and SAT tests have a fee, which you will find on the relevant web sites. (See below.)

ACT

The ACT (formerly known as American College Testing – www.actstudent.org and www.act.org '*is an achievement test based on knowledge for US higher education*'. It consists of four separate multiple-choice sections that measure English, Math, Reading and Science, and the score range is 1-36. There is no penalty for incorrect answers so you are encouraged to answer every question even if you're guessing. There is also an optional Writing Test some colleges require, so if you're not decided on your chosen college it's best to take it – the web site has a searchable list of colleges that have informed ACT whether or not they require results from the Writing Test:

★ The ACT web site's national average scores and scores reported by state are available at – http://www.act.org/newsroom/data/2012/states.html. The average ACT score in the USA is typically around 21 (out of a possible 36) but what is considered an average score at one college may not be good enough for another. The top schools tend to accept students with ACT scores in the 90th percentile, that is, a 28 and above. If your test score is lower, it must be balanced with a very good high school academic record.

★ The ACT tests are taken in one sitting and can be sat more than once. As you are allowed to send in your *single highest* ACT composite score on your application, most students take the ACT more than once (unless they get a high first score they believe they won't be able to beat). Even if the second or third attempts achieve a lower score than the first, you are still allowed to submit only the first score. Be aware your overall ACT score will be sent, not a specific sub-score. Some colleges, such as Yale and the University of Pennsylvania, ask to see all your ACT scores.

★ The ACT composite score is the average of the four sub scores during a single test, rounded to the nearest whole number. Your sub scores are meaningful in that if you think you can improve, for example, the Math score, it is worth trying again. However, although the Math score might improve with a further attempt, another sub-score might go down. For information about ACT scores, see the web site – www.act.org/aap/infosys/scores.html. (See below for more information on Reporting Scores and *superscoring*.)

★ There are ACT test centers around the world. Visit the ACT web site to find your closest test center. If you are not planning to take the ACT in the USA you must create an account and register online. The web site warns that not all test dates are available at every overseas location. If there is no test center within fifty miles of your home, the ACT organization may be able to provide 'arranged administrations' to enable you to take the test. The web site provides detailed guidelines on eligibility and how to make a request.

★ The ACT board will submit your test scores to colleges once you have directed them to do so. (See below, 'Reporting your scores'.)

★ ACT fees are listed on the web site – www.act.org. There is a basic fee with a small additional fee for the Writing Test, and an international surcharge which is not the same for every country. There is also a charge for changing the date or location of the test. Keep checking the web site as the fees do change.

★ As of October 2012, ACT requires all students to pre-register for tests, to upload a photo with registration, and to provide photo ID on arrival at the test center. Although you need not upload a photo at the time of registering, there is a deadline by which you must do this. Failure to upload a photo by this deadline cancels your test registration. Visit the relevant web page for complete details – http://www.act.org/newsroom/announce/testprocedures.html

SAT

The SAT is administered by the College Board – http://sat.collegeboard. org. It is a multiple-choice test and measures students in three areas – critical reading, writing (short essay and multiple choice), and Math. The overall score is out of 2400 and is broken down:

★ Writing – 200-800
★ Math – 200-800
★ Critical Reading – 200-800

Wrong answers are penalized a quarter of a point to discourage guessing. There are also subject tests you can take to demonstrate academic strength in particular areas. Some colleges require subject test scores and others do not:

★ The national average scores are Writing – 510, Math – 520, Critical Reading – 508. Remember the top colleges require much higher scores and will state the requirements, as well as previous class profiles, on their web sites.

★ There are over 1000 SAT test centers around the world and tests are offered six times per year (October, November, December, January, May and June). If you live more than 121 km (75 miles) from a test center, you can request a temporary test center be set up closer to you. Visit the College Board web site for all information on SAT testing.

★ There are several 'International exceptions and notices' posted on the SAT web site, highlighting different requirements for some countries. Make sure to read everything on the 'International' page as these exceptions cover fees, registration, and identification matters.

★ If you hear mention of SAT 1, it's the general SAT test, also known as the SAT Reasoning Test. The 20 *Subject Tests* used to be called SAT 2s and are sometimes still referred to like that. If you have specific colleges in mind, check whether they require an SAT Subject Test score in your application – also check to see if they accept substitutes such as English A Levels. (See 'Reporting your Scores' below, for more information.)

★ Fees – there is a basic SAT fee plus additional fees for specific subject tests (SAT 2s). The additional fees differ depending on the subject test taken but are clearly indicated on the web site – http://sat.collegeboard.org/register/intl-services-fees.

★ As with the ACT there are additional fees if you change the time or place of your test and if you are applying as an international student.

★ According to the College Board web site: '*For international students, it's important to take the exams two years before you expect to enter university. If you are one year away from when you expect to enter university, make sure to register for the SAT no later than the November before you plan to start your studies.*'

★ The web site has a specific PDF for international students with clear explanations and links for understanding the SAT program – http://sat.collegeboard.org/SAT/public/pdf/sat-program-student-brochure-international.pdf.

Although most colleges accept both tests for applications, the tests are slightly different in style. Some people believe the ACT English is easier than the SAT component, but as the ACT Math section includes Trigonometry, that part could be considered the more difficult of the two.

> **WARNING**
> If you have not studied Math for several years you may need tutoring to get up to speed.

Historically SAT questions are less straightforward than ACT questions, requiring practice in deciphering what is being asked. Fortunately both test boards have comprehensive web sites where you can download the latest sample test questions on which to practice. If you have no preference between ACT or SAT, consider taking both and sending in your best scores.

How to decide between ACT and SAT?

If you really can't decide, or you perform equally in both, there is nothing preventing you from taking both the ACT and SAT and sending in the better score, or sending in both scores. Foreign students however, may be limited by the location of test centers. Other ways to help you make your decision are:

★ Assess your own skills and what kind of a test-taker you are. The ACT and SAT are two very different types of test.

★ Kaplan, a test preparation company, has a 90-minute test combining ACT and SAT type questions designed to help you discover your preferred test – http://www.kaptest.com/pdf_files/college/sat-act-practice-test.pdf. Also – www.math.com/students/Kaplan/satoract.html gives a snap shot of both tests and explains the differences clearly.

★ Visit the ACT and College Board web sites, download practice tests in both exams and look at your scores.

★ The SATs Concordance table (on the web site) allows you to compare your ACT and SAT scores.

★ If you have specific colleges in mind, visit their web sites to see if they state a preference – the vast majority do not.

★ Where colleges accept both test scores, look at the minimum requirements for each test. Some colleges may have a higher minimum score for one test over the other. Also look at the range of scores of accepted students. In some instances the range for one test might be lower then the other test.

★ Find out whether the college in question *superscores* applicants' scores (see below). This may give you an advantage, as they will be taking your best sub-scores from individual tests rather than an overall score from only one sitting.

ACT and SAT tests are very different from many high school tests around the world. While you'll hear of some kids who walked into their test and got a perfect score, most entrants have been practicing for months. The bulk of the tests are multiple-choice, where the student is required to fill in the correct circle with an HB pencil. Easy as these tests may sound, some of the options are deliberately similar making the questions trickier than they appear. All tests are timed and some sections, such as the ACT Science section, require you to read seven passages and answer 40 questions in 35 minutes. Make sure you download some practice tests before the real thing to avoid unpleasant surprises.

Reporting your scores

Colleges requiring ACT/ SAT scores will ask you to have them sent directly to them by the relevant examining body. On both ACT/ SAT web sites there is a user-friendly explanation of how to have your scores sent to a specific college. In both cases, be sure to build in the time it takes for scores to reach your chosen colleges as it usually takes weeks:

★ **ACT score reporting**. According to the ACT web site, colleges are now using ACT scores in a variety of ways – www.act.org/aap/ infosys/scores.html:
  - The *single highest* composite score, which takes your highest ACT composite score from one test sitting (known as an *administration*).
  - The *most recent* composite score, which is the composite score of the last ACT test you sat.
  - The *combined highest*, which takes the best sub-scores over more than one test sitting, and often gives you a higher score. This is often called superscoring.
  - The ACT does not recommend any particular method and does not facilitate combining scores. Its official definition of a composite score remains: ' *…an ACT composite score is the average of the four multiple-choice scale scores from a single administration (test).'*
  - Here is an up-to-date list of colleges that superscore ACT subscores – http://www.collegeadmissionspartners.com/ college-testing/colleges-superscore-act/.

Your ACT scores are usually posted online around two and a half weeks after you take the test. They are reported to your high school (if authorized) and selected colleges within three to eight weeks after the test date. The Writing Test score is reported slightly later. You cannot cancel a report request by any method – www.actstudent. org/scores/report-descriptions.html.

★ **SAT score reporting**. Your test scores will be sent to colleges and available to you online two to three weeks after you take the test. The College Board estimates it will take about five weeks to have your score report sent to you and your high school if you have submitted the code:

- The tab 'Receiving Scores' on the SAT web site gives exact dates of score availability and mailing if you have requested a paper copy.

- You will be able to access your scores online through your College Board account. Scores by phone are released at the same time, for a fee and only with your test registration number, birth date, credit card number and expiration date. This service doesn't allow you to have scores sent to colleges any earlier.

- There have been recent changes in the options available when reporting SAT scores to colleges. Traditionally, if you reported SAT scores colleges could see scores from every SAT test you took, good or bad. Many colleges however, practiced *superscoring* whereby they took your highest sub-scores to get a combined *superscore* – usually higher than your composite test scores. The College Board gives a PDF list of colleges that *superscore*, called *Score use practices by participating institutions*.

- Score Choice™ is a new option for reporting SAT scores, where students can choose which scores to report, by test date and by individual Subject Test. The entire test score is sent with Score Choice and not individual test section scores. If you want to use Score Choice™ make sure your desired college allows it – you can find a list of participating colleges on the College Board web site, as well as more details about Score Choice™. If you opt not to use Score Choice™ all your SAT scores will be sent automatically to the colleges you specify.

⚠ **WARNING**
Score Choice™ sends your chosen scores to four colleges for free, but you will still not see them first. According to the College Board customer service representative I

spoke to, you have a nine day grace period after each test to decide whether to send in that particular score. Your decision is based on how you think you performed in the test. You can also wait till you know your scores and pay the fee to have them sent later.

The College Board web site contains a PDF on score practices by college – http://professionals.collegeboard.com/profdownload/sat-score-use-practices-list.pdf.
- You can cancel SAT scores within a few days of taking a test if you don't think you did well. These scores can't be reinstated and will not be reported to you or any college.

★ **ACT and SAT**. Whether you're taking the ACT or SAT you should bear the following in mind:
- Scores are not released to colleges automatically – you must make it happen. With both bodies you can name up to four colleges when you register to take the test. At your request your test scores will be sent to these colleges for no extra fee. You can have scores sent to other colleges, for a fee, at a later date. Note – these scores are sent to the colleges before you have seen them yourself, so if you want to wait till you know your scores you will have to forego this free service and have scores sent at a later date, for a fee.
- Send your score results in as soon as you can. The College Board states: '*In a recent survey, colleges said that receiving score reports is important to them because it shows which students are interested in their schools.*'
- Requests for additional reporting are processed a week after the request is received.
- Both SAT and ACT offer *rush reporting* for a fee, but check the college in question accepts this before having it done, and ask whether it's even necessary. Be aware your *application* deadline isn't necessarily a deadline for reporting scores from either body.

It is particularly important to understand your colleges' policies on this matter when you are applying ED (Early Decision) or EA (Early Action).

- Colleges receiving your test scores can take a week or more to process them once they are received. Another duration to factor into your overall planning.
- Use the valid college codes provided.
- Make sure you specify the campus to which you are applying if the college has more than one.
- If you are applying to more than one school at the same college, make sure your scores are going to both schools. This may be classed as reporting twice.
- Do not omit any identifying information (such as test ID) otherwise your report will be delayed.
- You may take a calculator into the Math section of the test but each web site has a list of prohibited types of calculator.
- In addition to prohibited calculators they also specify other items you may not take into the testing venue, such as cell phones and iPods. Even if you are not using them, if they are found in your pocket or in a bag, your test will be immediately voided.

Unsolicited test preparation calls

Organizations other than those you have registered with may find your contact information and call or e-mail regarding test preparation services. The College Board states it does not sell your personal information and cautions students against signing up with test prep companies if they did not initiate the communication. Never give out credit card information to these companies. If you are interested in their services, ask for a name and telephone number so you can call them back and check them out with the Better Business Bureau – www.bbb.org.

Accommodations

Students with physical or learning disabilities may be eligible for various *accommodations* when taking standardized tests. Accommodations include extended time, an exam reader, wheelchair accessibility, the use of a computer, and a quiet room. Visit the ACT and College Board web sites for details on eligibility and how to apply. Consideration of applications can take months, so factor this time into your overall planning. You can appeal a decision by sending additional information as requested by the examining body. No time extensions are given for test-takers who don't speak English as their first language, and the tests are not offered in any other language.

Chapter Seven
Offers and Rejections

The great thing about American college applications is (in most cases) you'll get a solid offer. Even when accepting predicted exam results an offer is not conditional on future results, although there is an understanding your grades won't plummet after the offer and acceptance. This is known as the *senior slide* or *senioritis* in the USA and offers can be rescinded if your final results fall considerably below predictions. This policy is usually clearly stated on college web sites such as the University of Colorado, Denver's site: '*The records of students whose grades drop significantly will be sent to the Admissions Committee for appropriate action, whether that be a warning letter, placement on probation, or retraction of admission. Therefore, it is important that you continue to do well academically.*'

There are a few situations where the offer might not be quite what you wanted (see below). Whatever the case, there are still a few more things on your to-do list before you set sail:

★ Before official offers or rejections are sent out you may receive a *likely letter* from a college, expressing interest in you. Not all colleges send these, but they are meant to make you think favorably about that college. If you are really interested in the college in question, acknowledge the letter but you are not usually required to, and it should never be taken as confirmation you have been offered a place there.

★ If you have applied to more than one college, you should wait till you hear from them all before making any decisions. In rare cases a college may require you to accept its offer before you've heard from other colleges. This is a difficult decision and you should weigh up the pros and cons, as well as the likelihood of getting into the college(s) you're still waiting to hear from. As mentioned in *Chapter Five – The College Application Process*, many colleges subscribe to the CRDA (Candidates' Reply Date Agreement), whereby they commit to giving you until the regular May 1 deadline to accept or decline an offer.

★ Don't turn down a college offer until you know the hand you've been dealt. Even if you've been told you'll definitely be accepted somewhere, wait until you have the offer in your hands before declining any others.

★ If you're holding more than one offer and are having trouble deciding, read the offer letters carefully. Many colleges award merit-based financial scholarships with their offers – this could make a significant difference to your annual costs and may tip the scales in favor of one college over another.

★ Go back to the notes you made about each college and make sure the offers you have are meeting your needs and wants. If you've been considering a few colleges it's possible you'll forget the details, so a reminder of what you liked and disliked might help you reach a decision.

★ If you are holding equally impressive offers and can't decide, try to talk to professionals in your areas of interest to see if one college is preferable in the relevant industry.

Deferrals and wait-listing

Deferred

You may get a solid offer from a college to start the following January, or spring semester. This is more common with smaller colleges as they try to fill spots from students who transfer or drop out. Remember, being deferred is still an offer and once you pay your deposit you have a place there. Some students might not like this offer as they feel they'll be behind other students in the freshman year, but there are ways to catch up before you start:

★ You may be able to take online tests for college credit. CLEP is the College-Level Examination Program run by the College Board (who also administer the SAT test) – http://clep.collegeboard.org/. According to the web site, CLEP is the most widely accepted credit-by-examination program, available at more than 2900 colleges and universities. For a much smaller fee than a semester's tuition, you can take one of a variety of CLEP tests and gain hours of college credits.

★ As acceptance of CLEP credentials and minimum requirements differ from college to college, you are advised not to take any exams until you have established their worth at your colleges of interest. Some colleges do not give credit for classes not taken on their own campus.

★ Summer school – many deferred students take classes over the summer to catch up with their peers.

★ Don't forget to ask whether your high school exam results (e.g. IB or A Levels) earn you credit hours, which may help you catch up with other freshmen if you're deferred till January or spring. Many international students arrive at US colleges with a full semester of credits under their belt so a spring start isn't the end of the world.

Wait-listed

Discussion web site *College Confidential* describes the wait-list as '*the nasty first cousin of deferrals*'. A college will wait-list you if they have made the maximum number of offers to applicants, but still want a reserve list in case someone declines an offer – effectively an insurance policy enabling the college to fill its freshmen spots. This isn't a rejection and it means there could be a place for you, but many colleges wait-list over a 1000 applicants and make offers to very few off that list:

★ **How many applicants are on wait-lists?** In recent years colleges have increased the size of their wait-lists, but in general the percentage of applicants taken from the wait-list is small. Some professionals, such as Lynn O'Shaughnessy (Higher Ed journalist and consultant), advise turning down a wait-listed offer and moving on – http://www.cbsnews.com/8301-505145_162-57527951/college-wait-lists-growing-in-popularity/.

★ **When will I know if I have been accepted?** Most colleges do not turn to their wait-lists until all offers have been accepted or rejected, which is usually in May (for a fall intake). It may take until August 1 to find out if they have gone to the wait-list and are offering you a place. As many colleges require you to accept or reject offers by the May 1 deadline, you may find yourself in the position of having to turn down a confirmed offer and gamble on a wait-listed place. Wait-lists are very difficult to predict so you are advised not to pin your hopes on getting into a college that has wait-listed you.

★ **Effect on visa application of being on a wait-list**. Being wait-listed is fairly common but a lot of hassle – you don't know where you're going until some months later than most other applicants. As the college you eventually accept will generate the I-20 (which you need before you can begin your visa application), the wait-list situation could seriously delay your start date.

There are several things you can do when faced with the dreaded wait-list offer:

★ Find out if the wait-listed offer will negatively affect any scholarships you are seeking, housing opportunities, and your chances of getting into a particular school or department.

★ If you want to stay on the wait-list, return the reply card or otherwise let the college know if you'd like to stay on, and do it by the deadline they have stated.

★ Try to find out how many wait-listed places the college has offered and what your chances are of getting in. Some colleges rank the wait-list and may tell you where you place on the list. Some colleges traditionally offer few spots to wait-listed students (because no one turns them down), while others are able to accommodate more. Unfortunately this number changes from year to year and colleges cannot make predictions.

★ Contact the Admissions office, or your regional representative, to demonstrate your continued interest in the college. Without being a nuisance let them know why you'd be a good match for the college and why you really want to go there. When filling spots from the wait-list they are still looking for applicants who are most likely to accept the offer.

★ Don't ask the Admissions office why you were wait-listed. Sometimes it may just be a numbers game. A more diplomatic question is to ask what more you can tell them about yourself.

★ If there is any positive change in your academic or extra-curricular history, let them know. Be careful not to repeat what is already in your application.

★ Re-evaluate. Think how much this college offer would mean to you. Are you prepared for months of not knowing where you are going to college? Is the second choice college somewhere you could see yourself? If there is very little difference in your first and second choice colleges, is it worth risking everything to get into the first college? Bear in mind if you do get a late offer from your first choice, you may not have the housing and financial aid options that would have been available earlier in the process.

★ If you haven't moved off a wait-list by May 1, one strategy is to enroll at your second-choice college (assuming you have an offer) while waiting, and pay the non-refundable deposit.* This will ensure you have a place in the freshman class at some college, and it also means you can begin your visa application process with the I-20 this college generates. Holding out for a wait-listing college will change your plans at a late stage and will probably delay the entire process of applying for, and obtaining, a visa.

★ If you have your heart set on a particular college but don't want to risk hanging on to your wait-list position, remember you can always apply to transfer in a year or two. If this is your plan, make sure you'd be able to transfer some or all of your credit hours and work hard to obtain good grades for your transfer application.

★ If you decide you're not going to take up an offer if you move off the wait-list, let the college know immediately, otherwise you're taking a potential offer from someone else.

---

* This is known as *double-depositing*. Double depositing is generally frowned on by college administrators, and this is the only situation where it is tolerated. Accepting more than one college place is considered unethical as it leaves colleges with a level of uncertainty regarding their incoming freshman class, and deprives other applicants of a place at that college. Some colleges reserve the right to rescind an offer if they discover you have double-deposited, and your high school may refuse to send final transcript information to more than one college. The practice is also in violation of standards set out by the National Association for College Admissions Counseling (NACAC).

Accepting and declining offers

Accepting offers

When you decide to accept a college offer, pay attention to the deadline and let the college know you are accepting. This means, **submit the paperwork that is required** – a phone call, in most cases, won't be enough. Many Admissions offices are automated when it comes to processing paperwork and while missing this crucial deadline may not be the end of the world, it will cause serious headaches. Don't forget to send in your deposit to secure your acceptance. (See next chapter for what to do once you've submitted an acceptance.)

Declining offers

There are two schools of thought with regard to declining offers. The first is that it's a courtesy to let the colleges know. Obviously if you don't send back your acceptance within the specified deadline, they will know you're not interested. Letting them know earlier means they can offer the place (and perhaps the financial aid) to another applicant. On the other hand, declining before a deadline may burn that particular bridge should you change your mind in the days and weeks ahead. It is definitely not advisable to start declining offers before you have a firm offer you know you might accept.

Deferring offers

If your plans change and you want to attend college at a later date, you can ask to accept but defer your start date. If you have been offered any type of scholarship, ask whether this would still be part of the package and get everything in writing before you make a decision. Gap years are not too common in the USA so remember you will be at least a year older than your peers when you enroll at college.

Space Availability Survey

If you end up with no college offers there's still another option. Every year the NACAC (National Association of College Admission Counseling) puts out its *Space Availability Survey: Openings for Qualified Students* report on colleges that can accommodate applications after the May 1 deadline. There are often a surprising number of colleges to which you can still apply after this deadline.

Passport

If you weren't required to send in passport details with your application, now is a great time to either apply for a passport or to make sure your current passport is in order. You need to have at least six months remaining on it when you arrive in the USA to begin your studies. If you are applying for a passport during the summer allow extra time for this. You will not be able to apply for a visa without a valid passport.

Chapter Eight
Before You Go - Visa Application and Other Important Steps

As already stated, the most important thing is to **send in your acceptance of a college offer** and pay the deposit or *enrollment confirmation fee*, if required. Telling someone in Admissions you're 'definitely coming' is not sufficient. The deposit is non-refundable, but is applied toward your tuition and fees on enrolment. There may be other deposits required at this time, such as housing.

If you are applying for financial aid the college may waive or defer the *enrollment confirmation* fee, but you must confirm your intent to enroll. Until you have confirmed your offer your visa application process cannot begin. Once your offer is confirmed there are several things to do before you set off for college. The most important, obviously, is to start the application for a student (Non-Immigrant) visa, but there are also other college-related steps to complete:

★ Read every single piece of information your college sends to you either by e-mail or snail mail. Financial information may be sent to your parents, so remind them not to leave any mail unopened and to check e-mails regularly.

★ There is usually additional information required from you, so make sure you complete and return any forms as soon as possible. You will have important deadlines covering everything from class registration to accommodation, and they're not all the same. Failure to submit the paperwork will often result in a 'hold', which may prevent you from applying for housing or from registering for classes. There's usually no way around this requirement, and you can't 'leave it till later'.

Government requirements

The following information is available on the US government web sites listed below, and as rules and regulations frequently change you are strongly advised to visit the web sites for up-dates.

The requirements surrounding your visa application and eligibility are set by the US government not by your college, although the college's Admissions or International Students Office will usually be able to advise and assist you. The steps below are typical for most applicants but can change at any time, and additional steps may be required in some countries:

Step 1 – Formerly accept the offer from one college and decline offers from any other colleges
Step 2 – College generates I-20 form
Step 3 – Pay SEVIS I-901 processing fee
Step 4 – Apply for Non-Immigrant visa
Step 5 – Submit form DS-160 electronic application and payment
Step 6 – Non-Immigrant visa interview
Step 7 – Airport transit visa application (if required)

Each step of the SEVIS requirements (Student and Exchange Visitor Information System – www.ice.gov/sevis) are covered in detail. Canadian citizens do not need visas to study in the USA but must obtain an I-20. For details go to – http://canada.usembassy.gov/ visas/visas/student-and-exchange-visas.html.

📖 **FURTHER READING**
In October 2012, the US Department of Homeland Security (DHS) released new guidelines for some Haitian F1 visa applicants, which can be found here – http://studyinthestates.dhs.gov/2012/10/dhs-has-extended-special-relief-for-certain-haitian-students

Student and Exchange Visitor Information System requirements (SEVIS)

Step 1 – Accept/ decline offers

When you accept an offer from a US college, the college will generate an **I-20 Application Form,** which is required by the US government before a visa is granted.* If you accept more than one offer each

---

* VISA WARNING FOR SPORTS STUDENTS – If you intend to play D1 or D2 sports and have been offered financial aid, the NCAA states:

'*Under no circumstances should an international student-athlete be issued a Form I-20 with the expectation of financial support from the athletics office before the student has been certified as a final qualifier by the NCAA Eligibility Center or is determined to be a partial qualifier in Division II.*'

In other words, even if your college issues the I-20 and you obtain a student visa before you get NCAA certification, you should not arrive at college. Should the NCAA find you ineligible you would be out of status and could be sent home.

college will generate an I-20 application form, so you must commit to one college only (and remember to decline the others) in order to proceed with your visa application.

The I-20 is specific to your college and is used by the US government to determine that you can finance your college degree. Information about fees for your particular college should be included in the I-20 application instructions. At this point you will need a valid passport. Do not plan to enter the USA on a business or tourist visa because you will not be able to start your studies under that classification.

When completing the I-20 application, the codes for majors comply with the US Department of Education codes and might not be those used by your college. If you can't find a code similar to a major you have chosen, call your International Students Office for assistance.

Step 2 – College will generate I-20

After determining you can fund your degree the college will mail you a paper copy of the I-20 and is responsible for entering the I-20 information into the Department of Homeland Security's system. Processing your I-20 could take several weeks.

As soon as you receive your I-20 paper copy, check it matches your passport and is signed by the DSO (Designated School Official) from your college. You cannot begin your visa application with incorrect information. **If anything is wrong, contact the college and have them issue another I-20**.

Do not lose this paper form as it will contain a specific SEVIS ID number (beginning with the letter 'N') which you will need. It is not advisable to begin the visa application process until you are told the paper I-20 is on its way to you. You cannot be interviewed without an I-20.

> ✔ **TIP**
>
> If you have the I-20 sent by an international parcel company such as FedEx or UPS, you will receive a tracking number to follow its progress to your college.

Step 3 – Pay SEVIS I-901 processing fee

The US Department of Homeland Security (DHS) requires all international students to pay a SEVIS I-901 processing fee for visa applications. Check the web site for up-to-date pricing – https://www.fmjfee.com/i901fee/index.jsp

★ Colleges may pay the SEVIS I-901 fee for the student but they are not required to and you should not assume this has been done. If your college pays the fee for you, you should get a receipt or proof of payment for your visa application. If the US college you are attending changes before your visa application, take the old SEVIS payment receipt and the new I-20 to your visa interview. If the fee is the same or greater, this payment will still be accepted. You should only have to pay the fee once.

★ Some colleges charge a fee for processing your SEVIS information – this isn't the same as the official SEVIS I-901 fee. Other colleges may pay all your SEVIS fees. Whatever the situation always make sure the official SEVIS I-901 payment has been made.

★ You will need the information from your I-20 form when paying.

★ You can pay the SEVIS I-901 fee online at – www.FMJfee.com, by mail or by a third party in the USA (your sponsor or your college if they do this for you). If you pay online make sure you are connected to a printer. You cannot leave and return to the page, nor can you print the coupon or payment receipt at a later time, and you will need this piece of paper for future steps in your visa application process.

★ DO NOT send cash as payment.

★ The SEVIS I-901 payment is recorded in the government system. You can schedule a visa interview before the money is deposited, but your interview cannot occur until the payment is confirmed in the SEVIS system. The interviewing officer will have access to the system and will be able to verify this. When you receive a receipt for the payment, either online or in the mail, keep it safe and take it to your visa interview.

★ According to the US government web sites failure to make any payments will result in a fraud alert against your name. On attempting to enter the USA you will be issued a Form I-515, allowing you 30 days to remit your SEVIS I-901 fee. If this happens, your college DSO should be able to help you.

📖 **FURTHER READING**
For all SEVIS questions refer to –
http://www.ice.gov/sevis/i901/faq.htm

Visa application process
According to the US government most applications are processed within days, but you are still advised to give yourself plenty of time. Many US embassy web sites around the world can give you up-to-the-minute estimates of visa application wait times.

 TIP
Some colleges/ staff members offer assistance with this and there are consulting companies who can oversee the whole process, for a fee.

Step 4 - Apply for Non-Immigrant visa

With the receipt for your I-901 SEVIS payment you can apply to the nearest American embassy or consulate for a student visa. The US government web site has a list of embassies and consulates around the world with links – http://www.usembassy.gov. Visit the web site of your nearest embassy or consulate in addition to the main US government web sites – http://travel.state.gov and http://studyinthestates.dhs.gov.

Here you can find details of how to start your application and how to schedule an interview. If you are experiencing trouble scheduling an interview, many embassies and consulates have procedures to expedite the process, so check the web site or phone to ask about it:

★ You will be applying for a student visa, which comes under the umbrella of a Non-Immigrant visa – category F for regular undergraduate students, and M for vocational (i.e. graduate/ PhD) students. If you are on any type of exchange program this will require a J visa.

Step 5 - Submit form DS-160 electronic application and payment

Use the online Form DS-160 electronic application to apply for your Non-Immigrant visa. The information you submit will be used to decide on your visa application – any corrections may lead to the visa interview being rescheduled. The government web site has FAQs and instructions about this form – http://travel.state.gov/visa/forms/forms_4401.html:

★ To complete this electronic form you will need:
  - Passport
  - Digital photo to upload
  - Travel itinerary, if available

- Dates of previous visits to the USA and possibly information on other international travel
- Résumé/ CV
- SEVIS ID from the I-20 form
- Name and address of the college you plan to attend
- Additional information relevant to your application which you will be advised of by your embassy or consulate

★ Don't forget the electronic signature at the end of the form.

★ Do not hit the 'submit' button until the form is complete. You can pause and save, but you need your ID number to return to the form and you must return to it within 30 days. After online submission print the confirmation page with the barcode. **You will need this barcode for all future steps in your visa application**.

Step 6 – Non-Immigrant visa interview

Once you have submitted your DS-160, you should contact your local US embassy or consulate for instructions on how to arrange a visa interview – www.usembassy.gov. There may be specific instructions for your country or region.

Some embassies do not require you to schedule an interview and will ask you turn up and stand in line – some have strict instructions regarding how early you need to arrive before your interview. In preparation for your visa interview make sure all paperwork contains exactly the same spelling of your name and other relevant information:

★ You will also need to take:
  - Appointment confirmation letter
  - I-20 form
  - Confirmation of DS-160 application and assigned bar code
  - Passport, valid for at least six months after your arrival at college

- Receipt for visa processing fee, paid prior to interview
- SEVIS 901 payment receipt
- Proof of funding for amounts listed on the I-20 form. Make sure you fully understand how your education is being paid for – some embassy officials will ask what impact this payment will have on the family you leave behind or how your second and subsequent years will be financed
- Other documentation as required by your interviewing officer, such as proof of ties to your country of origin, academic credentials, standardized test results (SATs, TOEFL etc.), and the original letter of admission from your college
- Photo taken within the last six months, if relevant

This list may not be exhaustive – check with the local US embassy/consulate before your interview.

★ Your visa interview will be conducted in English.

★ Do an Internet search for 'F1 visa questions' and you will discover examples of questions from students who have been through a visa interview. You should be able to clearly articulate:
- **Why you want to study in the USA** and why you have chosen your college over others. Be prepared to talk in depth about your academic interests and what your college offers in that area.
- **What you plan to do after finishing your degree**. You must be able to convince the interviewer you plan to return to your home country and put your degree to good use.
- **Who is sponsoring your studies** and how you plan to cover each year of your degree.

Make sure you have all your test scores with you, and that you understand and can explain all paperwork relating to how you will finance your studies.

★ Don't tell lies in your interview – if you are discovered lying you may be permanently denied a visa. If you are unsure of an answer, better to admit this. If you are then denied, you will at least be able to appeal or apply again.

★ Don't submit fake paperwork. Even if your local US embassy or consulate grants you an F1 visa, the US government might decide, when reviewing your paperwork, that something is amiss. In such cases applicants have been called back to the local embassy and the visa canceled.

★ Your visa may be denied because of lack of documentation or failure to demonstrate eligibility (e.g. '*insufficient ties to home country*'). This doesn't mean you can't reapply and you should be given a reason for the denial together with a list of additional information required.

★ The US Consular body advises you not to purchase a non-refundable travel ticket until your visa has been issued.

★ Your visa does not guarantee entry into the USA. You may still be denied entry by a CBP (Customs and Border Protection) officer at your port of entry to the USA.

★ After being granted a Non-Immigrant visa, your SEVIS document will show the latest date you can report to your college. It will not be possible to enter the USA after this date.

Visa information

After your visa interview, you should bear in mind the following:

★ Although first-time students in the US cannot enter the country earlier than 30 days before classes start, you can hold your visa for 120 days before this date. If you apply earlier than this 120-day period, the embassy/ consulate will delay processing your application until the correct date.

> ⚠ **WARNING**
> If you need or want to enter the US earlier than the 30-day period you must apply for a visitor visa. Before beginning your studies you must obtain approval for a change in status (filing form I-539) and pay a fee. You cannot begin your studies without this change of classification.

Continuing students (i.e. those who are not beginning their first year) may enter the US at any time provided they have maintained status and their SEVIS records are intact and up-to-date:

- Some visa applications will require *further administrative processing* and applicants are told of this when applying – according to the government's web sites, in most situations the application query is resolved within 60 days of the visa interview, but applicants may not enquire about the decision before this time has elapsed.

★ Where visa applications undergo security clearances, some countries experience longer delays. Your college will not be able to intervene in this process. If such a delay threatens to cause you to miss your orientation or the start of classes, call your college as soon as this becomes apparent.

★ When you receive your student visa it will be in a sealed envelope attached to your passport. **Do NOT open this envelope – the official at the US port of entry must open it**.

★ The F1 visa is for travel purposes – to stay in the USA legally your I-20, I-94 and passport should all be valid.

★ To enter and re-enter the US your passport must be valid for at least six months after your arrival. If your passport expires but your visa is still valid, you should carry your old passport containing the visa, as well as your new passport, when traveling.

★ Expired visas cannot be renewed in the US, and you are advised to renew in your home country rather than a country adjacent to the USA in case there are delays. Check with your local US embassy/consulate for renewal details. When you leave the USA to renew your visa, you cannot re-enter until it is valid.

Step 7 – Airport transit visa application (if required)

Some countries require citizens of certain other countries to obtain an airport transit visa (ATV) if they are traveling through their territory. This sometimes applies even if such travelers will not leave the airport in question and you are usually not authorized to leave the airport:

★ A transit visa is issued by the embassy or consulate of the country through which you plan to travel. After you have decided on your flight options to the USA, talk to the airline about ATVs and double check with the relevant transfer country's embassy in your country.

★ There are two types of transit visas:
  - **Airside** – when you are changing flights in the same airport or terminal and do not need to go through immigration.
  - **Landside** – if you go through Immigration but get a second flight out within 24 or 48 hours. If you plan to spend more than this time in the country, you will need a regular tourist or visitor visa.

⚠ **WARNING**
Rules regarding transit visas change regularly, so don't rely on the advice of someone who may have made the same journey a year or two ago.

★ As the transit visa application usually requires proof of eligibility to travel on to the final destination, you will probably have to show proof of your US student visa or your I-20 form. This means you should not apply for your transit visa first.

★ You are advised not to purchase a ticket until you have your transit visas, but you may be required to show proof of a reservation to obtain this visa. Check with the airport in question and your airlines.

★ Transit visas may also be referred to as 'Schengen' visas, but they are not always the same. There are currently 26 Schengen countries in Europe requiring some travelers to obtain a Schengen visa to enter or travel through them, but other countries also require them. Refer to the web site for information on Schengen countries – http://www.schengenvisa.cc/.

★ Because of the almost unlimited combinations of countries of origin, destination, and airport transfer, it is not possible to list all related web sites here. Type your query into an Internet search (e.g. 'India to USA transit visa requirements') or go to your airline's web site for help. Heathrow Airport has a web page which addresses transit visas and gives links to the UK Border Agency information – http://www.ukba.homeoffice.gov.uk/visas-immigration/transitthroughtheuk/.

Driving documentation

According to Amanda Ecklar of Yale University's Office for international Students and Scholars, "One of the biggest documentation omissions I see is students forgetting to obtain an International Drivers' Permit (IDP) before leaving their country of origin. Some states require this permit before giving you a local driver's license – if you require this document, it cannot be obtained once you are in the USA. Rules regarding required driving documentation differ from state to state – if you wish to obtain a US driving license it must be obtained from the state where you will attend college."

> **📖 FURTHER READING**
> Visit the US government web site for comprehensive details on drivers' permits for the USA – http://www.usa.gov/Topics/Foreign-Visitors-Driving.shtml

College requirements and preparation

As well as government requirements there will also be a number of items on your to-do list relating to your college.

Tuition payment

With most colleges, about a month before you start classes, your tuition, or a portion of your tuition, is due. If you are paying by wire transfer make sure you have the correct details from your college's web site.

Social networking

Although not a requirement it is a good idea to join the social network page for incoming freshmen at your college. The official college web site may direct you to Facebook pages, or you can do an Internet search. It will either be listed as 'Incoming Freshmen' or 'Class of… ', followed by your graduation year and college. Do this as soon as you accept the offer because some students will be ahead of you in their preparations and can save you much time and anguish with their advice and information. It also means you'll have some friendly faces to look for when you arrive in the States.

Academic advisor

All students are assigned an academic advisor before classes start. This individual's role is to advise you on academic matters such as class registration, workload and graduation requirements. Usually students are allocated their academic advisor after attending orientation, but before registration. At some colleges you will also be assigned an advisor for your school or department if that is relevant.

International students don't usually go through orientation until just before classes start. Where this is the case, you will get to know your academic advisor at this point and s/ he will assist you in putting your schedule together. If you are allowed to register for classes at an earlier time make sure you have been assigned an academic advisor and make contact with him/ her before registering. In some instances you may need his or her approval before registering for certain classes. (See next chapter for note on orientation.)

 TIP
If you attempt to contact your academic advisor with no luck, call the office or your specific school (such as Business or Engineering) or the International Students Office for assistance.

Holds

Most colleges require you to go through the pre-registration steps in a particular order and will place a 'hold' on your application if you miss one of these steps. For example, you may not be able to register for orientation or for classes until you have submitted the required health forms (see below). It is also common to be blocked from registering for classes until you have completed your housing application and paid your tuition deposit. This varies from college to college, but if you see the word 'hold' against your name it's because you've neglected a vital step.

Housing

Once you have accepted an offer you will usually be allowed to apply for accommodation. There are generally many options for housing at American colleges and you should read the web site carefully, together with student comments and blogs that are often available. Your housing application will have a deadline after which time you will be assigned what's left. If you are asked to give three choices don't think if you only give one option you are guaranteed to get that dorm – you are more likely to get something that is tenth on your list:

★ **Freshmen Housing**. Most colleges require freshmen to live on campus, which means to live in a Residence Hall. In addition, many dorms are specifically for freshmen only, so your choices may be limited to those dorms.

✔ **TIP**
While the accommodation might be formally referred to as a Residence Hall, students speak of 'dorms' rather than 'halls' for the most part.

★ **Housing Communities**. More and more colleges are offering housing communities where students hoping to major in the same disciplines, or who have similar interests, can reside together. The reason is that you will probably have to take required (core/ pre-requisite) classes before embarking on your intended major, so you won't necessarily be meeting students with the same academic interest in your first year. There are very often dorms specifically for international students. The term for such housing differs from college to college – examples include special-interest housing, and living-and-learning housing. For housing with an academic bent, you may be required to *test in* or otherwise prove your eligibility.

★ **Fraternity/ sorority housing**. Although fraternities and sororities do have their own housing it is typically only available to sophomores and above. This is primarily because you won't be able to apply or *pledge* to a frat/ sorority until after you start at college. (See *Chapter Nine – On Arrival* for more about pledging and the Greek life.)

★ **Honors housing**. If you have successfully applied to be an honors student, you may also be able to apply for honors housing, which is similar to the special interest housing mentioned above.

★ **If you don't like your housing arrangements**. If you are assigned housing that isn't to your liking, call the Housing office and ask if it's possible to switch. Some offices will have official wait-lists they can put you on, and in other colleges you will be expected to find someone who wants to switch with you. This is usually done through the student forums. Try to do some homework on the student accommodation before making your choice, as not being happy in the first few weeks of college only adds to an already stressful situation. Students' forums and chat rooms are often great places to learn about the various dorms at your college.

★ Sharing dorm rooms. The norm in the US is for students to share a dorm room with at least one other person. This means there are less single rooms available, but if you want a single room there might not be as much competition for them.

Roommate(s)

In most American colleges sharing with another student is the norm and there are sometimes larger rooms with a group of students living together. If you can't face the thought of sharing a room (and some of those rooms are quite small), make this known to the Housing office.

If you are planning to share a room, there are several ways you can do this:

★ **Selecting a roommate**. Some colleges allow you to select your own roommate. If you have a good friend who's enrolling at the same time, you can apply to be roomies. In most cases the college will require both of you to select each other independently.

★ **Online forums for roommates**. Some incoming freshmen put the word out on student forums (even Facebook), conduct a kind of speed-dating ritual, and then agree with someone that they'd like to share a room. If you're considering doing this but aren't really sure, ask people who have done it in the past. You'll find roughly the same percentage of success and failure stories as you would with randomly selected roomies.

★ **Web sites for roommates**. There are many web sites where you can list yourself and look for a college roommate. Do a search on 'find a college roommate' and several such sites will come up.

★ **College questionnaire**. Many colleges offer a pairing up system, whereby you complete a questionnaire and they will pair you with a student they think will be a good match. Again, while it might give you something to talk about, it's not a guarantee of anything.

★ **Random/ surprise roommates**. Traditionally students turned up on day one to find someone sitting in their dorm room who would be there for the year. This is referred to as 'going potluck'. (The term 'potluck' usually refers to a party where all the guests bring something to eat, so the connection with college rooming is tenuous.) Even if you go for the surprise element you will probably be told each other's names before college starts. This means you can make Internet contact before you meet, so there should be a comfort level going in.

★ **However you find your roommate**, contact them before arrival to discuss what you are both bringing to college. There's no point in both of you supplying an electric kettle (if they're allowed) or a full-length mirror.

In general, unless you've pre-arranged something, the student who arrives at the dorm room first gets to pick his/ her bed.

As an international student attending orientation right before classes start, you may be able to take up residency in your allocated dorm room during this time. Other colleges require you to stay in hotel accommodation until the official start of the semester. In such cases they will have recommendations for hotels on or near your campus. Make sure you clarify these arrangements with your college and if required to book into a hotel, don't leave it till the last minute.

Off-campus accommodation

If you are not planning to live on campus many college web sites have information on local housing options, often with lists of current availability. Amanda Ecklar, of Yale University's Office for International Students and Scholars, states, "We strongly advise against signing any type of lease for non-affiliated housing before you have seen it, as it is often very difficult to get out of a lease once it's signed."

Move-in

Moving hundreds or thousands of students into dorms at the start of the school year is an enormous challenge and requires careful management. Most colleges now have *move-in* down to a fine art with scheduled slots and an army of student volunteers to help.

As an international student who will probably be attending orientation before classes start, you may be able to move into your dorm room while you attend orientation. If so you will still need to contact your college and arrange the specific time you would like to move in. College officials will tell you when and where to pick up your key or card to access your dorm building and dorm room.

Although every college has a different way of moving new students in, make sure you have answers to the following questions:

★ Do I have a dorm allocation?
★ Do I have a room number?
★ How do I get my dorm and room key? (Will someone meet me at the dorm or am I to collect the key from a specific place?)
★ If I am having my possessions delivered, is there a specific time this has to happen? Many colleges require students to book a move-in slot so there aren't too many students trying to use the elevators or stairs at the same time.
★ If my possessions are being brought in a vehicle (either delivery or family car) is there somewhere close to the dorm to park?

Meal plan

Along with your housing application, you'll be required to sign up for a meal plan. (Some colleges don't give freshmen an option, unfortunately.) A meal plan is a pre-paid dining account where you deposit money and receive a meal card (like a debit card) to swipe whenever you use the college dining facilities. Most colleges require freshmen to eat on campus, although they typically offer various plans:

★ You may be required to purchase a certain amount of meals per week. If one option is to include breakfast, think carefully about the likelihood you'll get up in time to make the cafeteria for breakfast. (If you are allowed a mini refrigerator in your room, you could keep breakfast supplies there for the odd occasion you're up in time.)

★ Many meal plans will allow you to add funds to your account, but they won't give you a refund for money not spent. They may however, allow you to roll it over into the next semester.

★ Other dining cards don't require you to consume a specific number of meals per week, but debit purchases from your balance. There may be a minimum dollar amount you have to deposit at the beginning of each semester.

★ If you're lucky your college's dining card will allow you to eat at off-campus cafes and restaurants nearby. Sometimes these places are cheaper than the college cafeterias.

★ Be sure to look at the cafeterias included in the meal plan. If they are all on-campus, do they offer a variety of food? Some of the colleges I have visited seem to feed their students a constant diet of pizza and burgers, so if this isn't to your liking you should carefully consider your options.

★ Check the cost for two meals per day versus three meals per day. In some colleges it's exactly the same.

Orientation

Many US colleges hold several orientation sessions throughout the summer for incoming freshmen. Orientations session usually last two or three days and are designed to provide information about the college, help incoming students meet other students, and introduce them to the campus. As international students usually can't arrive more than 30 days before classes start, most colleges offer an international students' orientation session right before classes start. You may also have a school or department-specific orientation to attend in addition to the international student session:

★ Orientation procedures differ from college to college but international students are legally required to check-in with their college and be registered by them on the government SEVIS web site – www.ice.gov/sevis.

★ In some colleges you must sign up for this orientation course and in others there is no need as your presence is mandatory. Look for this information before making your travel plans and, if registration is required, make sure you are registering for the correct session. Most colleges have different sessions for international and transferring students. (See next chapter for more detailed information on orientation.)

★ If you are classed as a foreign student but have attended high school in the US, you may be able to attend regular orientation in the summer.

★ Some colleges with a larger number of international students hold regional orientations around the world. Your International Students Office will have details on this.

★ Organize your orientation accommodation before you arrive on campus. While some colleges allow you to occupy your assigned dorm room, many ask you to book into a nearby hotel. Don't leave it till the day before you leave to do this, as you may find every hotel in the area already fully booked. One or both parents often accompany American college freshmen when they first move in, and parents stay in neighborhood hotels. Colleges usually provide information about neighboring hotels and rental options on their web sites, but you can also find local accommodation by doing an Internet search.

★ With most colleges there is an orientation fee to pay, although it may be automatically included in your college fees.

Bank account

It makes sense to open a bank account in the USA as most banks offer free checking (which is your 'current', non-savings account), a debit card and online banking services. After that services differ from bank to bank so make a comparison before you choose one:

★ First, take a look at your college web site. There will be general advice on the closest banks, plus information on the services they offer. Many international student web sites will also give advice for non-Americans wishing to open a bank account.

★ Not all banks in the US are national, so make sure there is a branch of your bank near your campus. With most American banks, if you withdraw money from your own bank's ATM (cash machine) there is no charge, but if you use another bank's ATM there will be a charge of a few dollars for every withdrawal.

★ If your International Students Office recommends a particular bank, it is probably because that bank is more used to dealing with international money wiring, which may mean fewer problems occur.

★ It is also a good idea to ask your own bank (or your parents' bank) what they can do with regard to sending money to the US and how much they charge.

★ Foreign checks usually take four to six weeks to clear and there is also a processing fee. Travellers' checks are quicker to deposit and they should be in US dollars – most banks accept American Express travellers' checks so these are the safest to buy. Wire transfers of money and online transfers of funds are usually possible from and to anywhere, and take a few days to process. There is also a fee for this service. In all cases take your passport and another form of ID (student ID) with you when receiving or sending money at your bank.

A few things to consider when choosing a bank are:

★ Whether there is a minimum deposit amount or a minimum balance you must maintain – very few American banks allow overdrafts and if you bounce a check there is usually a charge.

★ Whether the bank accepts personal checks from foreign accounts and what the fees are (if this is your plan for funding).

★ Whether you can send and receive wire transfers and what the fees are.

★ How easy will it be to use travellers' checks? – many banks in smaller cities and towns have restrictions on what they will accept.

★ Will you be able to get a credit card? Some banks issue credit cards to students without a Social Security number, if there is a co-signor with a Social Security number and good credit history in the US.

★ Your US bank may issue you with a checkbook, although many students don't use them – checks can be used in some stores if accompanied by a photo ID such as a driving license or a passport. Most restaurants will not accept checks.

✔ **TIP**
The spelling is *check* and not cheque.

If it proves too difficult to set up a bank account from outside the USA, wait until you are in the country. Most banks will want to see proof of ID, proof of permanent residence and possibly visa papers too.

Health care

Health care in the United States is not free and most citizens have health care insurance to cover some, or all, health costs. When receiving medical care, the *provider* (the doctor or hospital) will either ask for payment on the spot, bill your health insurance company, or deduct the cost from your student account.

It is not advisable to skip health care insurance, and in most colleges it is mandatory to have coverage either under state law or through their own policies and procedures. You might think receiving treatment for minor ailments isn't worth worrying about, but one injury can quickly rack up thousands of dollars of costs:

★ If you don't have health care insurance covering your stay in the USA your college may offer student health insurance through one of the bigger American insurance companies. This will be covered comprehensively on the web site, but if you are unclear e-mail or phone the relevant department for assistance.

★ If you aren't used to private health care (i.e. not government provided) it might seem extremely confusing at first. Every health insurance company has customer service representatives to explain things to you, and most doctors, clinics, and hospitals will help you through the process too. Remember to keep every scrap of paper you receive relating to your health insurance claims and any treatment you might receive.

★ In some colleges you will automatically be enrolled onto their health insurance program unless you provide evidence of existing coverage under another health plan, such as your parents' policy. Make sure you establish whether this is the case as soon as possible. In most cases any coverage you may already have must be similar/ have the same levels of coverage as that offered by your college.

★ There are many non-US companies offering health insurance for students while they study in the USA. Compare their prices with what your college offers – student health care insurance premiums are often cheaper than 'regular' folks' policies, and colleges may be able to negotiate even deeper discounts on premiums. This is because the health insurers are covering a large pool of young, relatively healthy adults with limited payouts involved.

★ Pay attention to the coverage amount and what, specifically, is covered in the plan, for example *well visits* (checkups) and emergency room visits. Take into account the percentages you are expected to contribute. Some policies ask you to pay 20% of every bill, some have a *deductible* (excess) you must pay before they pay anything at all and others cover everything until a cap kicks in, after which you are responsible for all costs. **Read the small print and calculate the cost**.

★ Remember the maxim, '*If it looks too good to be true, it probably is*'. In general, the lower the monthly or annual premium, the less coverage you get. While most young adults don't have many ailments, one serious accident could cost hundreds of thousands of dollars, so make sure you are covered for a 'catastrophic' event.

★ Many colleges have their own student clinic where you may have to pay up-front for treatment received, as opposed to the clinic billing your health insurance provider. If this happens to you submit your paperwork to your health insurance provider after the treatment, if the policy covers the treatment.

★ If you think you won't need health insurance because you never get sick, think again. According to the American College Health Association – www.acha.org, in any given year:
  - 11.5% of students get strep throat
  - 6.9% succumb to an ear infection
  - 17.7% suffer sinus infections
  - 8.1% have broken noses or fractures
  - 1.6% end up with mononucleosis (glandular fever)
  - 21.2% of students are treated for allergies
  - 17.8% of all students have at least one mental health condition
  - 53% of student respondents in the 2011 report stated they had received treatment for a minor ailment (such as the above) in the previous twelve months

Most of these conditions require at least a trip to the student health center plus a prescribed medication, neither of which is free.

 WARNING

According to Amanda Eckler of Yale University's Office for International Students and Scholars (OISS), "It is essential to find out whether your treatment is covered by your health insurance **before** being treated. If your treatment is not included in your plan the amount is often automatically deducted from your student account. For many students such a deduction could cause major budgeting problems." Ms Ecklar also advises any students arriving before the official start of classes (e.g. for language courses) to make sure their student health insurance covers this period, as it often doesn't.

Immunization records

Although there are no federal (national) vaccination requirements, each state has laws relating to children and students from birth to age 18. With regard to college students some states have further legal requirements, others issue *recommendations* to colleges and still others leave it up to the individual colleges to specify required immunizations. Check on your college web site to learn which, if any, immunizations you must prove you have had. You will not be allowed to begin classes until you comply:

★ Online enrolment for classes (registration) obviously opens up before classes start, and if your college doesn't have your medical information in the system you may find yourself locked out (referred to as a 'hold').

★ As immunization laws vary from state to state you must get this information directly from your college. Typical requirements ask for vaccinations such as diphtheria, tetanus, pertussis, (DTP) measles, mumps and rubella (MMR), Hepatitis B, Polio and Chicken Pox. Don't rely on a friend in another state or another college for information as requirements differ and change regularly.

★ Depending on your country of origin you may be asked to show negative results of a Tuberculosis (TB) test, or to have the test administered once you arrive on campus.

★ Download the blank form from the college web site (often referred to as the *physical*) and take it to your doctor, who will be able to provide the information plus an official signature. Look over the form once your doctor has completed it and check all signatures and date requirements have been signed.

★ You may need a few vaccinations or boosters before you can submit the form. Don't leave it till the last minute to do this, as some vaccinations require two shots spaced a month or more apart.

★ If you have any questions whatsoever call the college for help, and call the Admissions office when you think they should have received the form, to make sure it contained everything that was required.

★ Your college may ask you to bring the physical form to your orientation session, so don't lose the original.

★ Many foreign students have found it pays to have all dental and vision check ups done in their home country before arriving in the USA, where it is usually more expensive.

★ If your country of origin does not provide immunization records to citizens, contact the college Admissions office for advice. In many instances you will be able to receive the required vaccines and tests on arrival in the USA. This may not be covered by your student health insurance, so check costs and method of payment beforehand.

Registration

In American colleges, you don't apply to study a specific subject and show up on the first day. College students are required to put their own syllabus and schedule together by choosing from the vast catalog of classes on offer. Signing up for classes is called 'registration' and it can be a nail-biting experience. Fortunately many colleges now offer online registration tutorials as well as support from advisors.

Where colleges have an orientation period for international students right before classes start, you will usually be able to register at this time. Because it happens during orientation, there will be people around to guide you through the process. Some international students may be required to register before arriving in the USA. If that is the case make sure you thoroughly understand the process before attempting to register.

If you have been allocated an academic advisor this is the person to contact, otherwise call the International Students Office or the school to which you have been admitted, such as the Engineering or Business school. If you already know an American student, ask him or her for advice as s/ he will be familiar with the process. Although they probably won't be able to tell you exactly which classes to register for, they will be able to explain how the process works and, hopefully, calm you down a little.

Whatever the mechanics of your registration, there are common points to note:

★ To register for classes you will need your college ID to log into the system. Make sure you have this well ahead of time so you can register when everyone else does.

★ Your college will give you a date and a specific time when you can go online and sign-up for classes. Usually registration opens up to seniors and juniors first. If the web site is open for freshmen at 7 am, you should try to get online at that time – delaying for even a few hours could mean you don't get your first choice classes, which in turn could render your whole schedule unworkable. (Think of it like a giant jigsaw puzzle.) Joe Holleran, a British student in Washington DC, learned the hard way when he didn't go online as soon as registration was open for him. Joe estimates that after the first five minutes 80% of his intended classes were already full, and he had to reorganize his schedule completely.

★ If you miss your allocated registration period you may find you're charged a fairly hefty late fee to be allowed to register.

⚠ **WARNING**
Remember there are four time zones in the USA. They are *Eastern* for the east coast, *Central* for the mid-west and half the central area, *Mountain time* for the west half of the central region and *Pacific* for the west coast. If your college opens up registration at a certain hour, make sure you understand which time zone they're using – www.worldtimezone.com/time-usa12.php gives information on world time zones.

Before registration is open read everything in the introduction to the list of classes, as this section will explain in plain English what you should be looking for. In most cases the web site will begin with a general overview of how many credits you'll need to graduate, and where these credits should come from (e.g. Sciences, Arts, Foreign Language, Writing, core classes, majors and electives.) Work with your advisor to draft a schedule and answer any questions.

Next, go through the class list on the web site (or perhaps in the catalog your college has sent you) and put together a draft schedule. Things you should be looking at are:

★ **Course load minimum**. This refers to the minimum number of credits or credit hours you must take. Colleges require a specific number of credit hours and your visa requires you to be enrolled as a full-time student. Each class you take will give you a specific number of these credits for the semester – add these up for your semester total and make sure it meets the minimum requirement. Most students take four to six classes per semester, and those classes each meet several times per week. Although you can take more than the regular course load, you may need authorization from your advisor and it might be a good idea to wait until you know how you handle the regular course load.

 WARNING

According to Amanda Ecklar of Yale University's Office for International Students and Scholars, one of the most common causes of deportation is students falling below the minimum course load requirement, often without realizing. International Student Offices are responsible for verifying your visa status is maintained and must inform the government if this is not the case.

★ **Distribution requirement**. Most colleges have a distribution requirement designed to give students a broad educational background. This is often referred to as Gen Ed (General Education) or your core classes. Students are required to take a minimum number of classes in several departments, schools or disciplines, (the terminology differs from one college to another). The list of disciplines typically includes Math, Sciences, Humanities, Writing/ English and sometimes a language, and there are usually many options to choose from. If you are enrolled at a particular 'school' within your college (e.g. Engineering or Business), your distribution requirements may be specific to that school.

⚠ WARNING

Although British student Joe Holleran found his Math and Economics classes were something of a step backwards for him, he found political and writing classes more difficult than expected. Because his British education had allowed him to narrow his studies down to three subjects in his final two years, it had been a long time since he'd had to read large amounts of text or write long essays and papers. Ask around if you're looking for less challenging freshman classes to take.

★ **Pre-requisite classes**. As well as the distribution requirement, as a freshman, you may have to consider pre-requisite classes when registering. Before you choose a class, check to make sure it doesn't have a pre-requisite class listed – if it does, you must register and pass that class first (or place/ test out of it). If you have a particular area of study you plan to concentrate on or major in, there will almost certainly be pre-requisite classes you must complete first. Before registering for such classes you should talk to your academic advisor about your intended major.

In most cases, when you click on a class to register, it will bring up the relevant pre-requisites too. In general, as you're not usually required to declare your major until the end of your second year, you will have time to take all your pre-requisites, but if you can knock some off the list in your first two years it could mean a lighter workload and less panic later on.

You usually don't have to cram all your required classes into the first semester, or even the first year, but in some cases you won't be able to take *elective* classes until you've completed the required ones. (Electives are classes that are not required by the college in order to graduate.) In some colleges you can take required classes at any time before you graduate, but think about whether you want to be taking your least favorite class when you're in your final year and you haven't looked at the subject for three years or more. Similarly if you take very easy classes for the first few semesters, you run the risk of having a tough time down the road fulfilling the more difficult requirements all at the same time. Try to find a balance in your classes.

★ **Restricted classes**. Some classes are restricted to students who have declared a major or a minor in a specific subject, or to students in a particular school within the college, such as Engineering, Business or Pre-med.

★ **Teaching style**. Although not an official college web site – www.ratemyprofessors.com is a widely used resource for students. With over 7,500 schools (higher education establishments) and over 13 million student-generated comments and ratings, this is a great resource for researching specific college classes and how they are taught. Professors are rated on helpfulness, clarity, 'easiness' and overall quality, making it possible to learn about teaching styles, homework loads and teaching assistants for each professor. If you have any doubts about a class you are considering, there may be additional information on this web site. You can also find information about colleges here.

★ **Placement tests**. Many subjects have beginner, intermediate and advanced level classes, and you may be required to take a placement test to determine which class to take. This has to be done before registering for the class, and in some colleges there is an early deadline of May or June to start classes in the fall. These tests are taken online and can take anything from 30 minutes to a couple of hours – colleges often have sample tests on the web site. If you scored particularly well in a high school subject that requires a placement test, your exam result may exempt you from the test and place you in a specific class automatically. If you have any questions, approach your academic advisor first.

★ **Language classes**. Many colleges require you to take a language, at least for the first semester or year. Don't worry, you can meet this requirement with an introductory class in almost every language on the planet. If you want to continue a language you've already studied, there may be an online placement test (see above) to help decide which class to take (intermediate, advanced, etc.).

Some colleges allow students to place/ test out of the language requirement by demonstrating foreign language competence in a number of ways – by taking a test to demonstrate the required standard or by having achieved a high score in high school examinations. If you have studied a particular language throughout high school for example, you should ask your academic advisor if you still need to take a required language class. Foreign students who have lived and studied in a country where English is not the first language may often petition that they can demonstrate foreign language competency.

★ **Science classes**. Although most colleges require their undergraduates to take some Science classes in order to graduate, if you know you are not going to major in a Science subject you can usually find classes specifically for non-Science majors. These classes will usually be less hard-core and quite wide in range. Many Science classes also have a placement test. If you are planning to study anything remotely scientific as a major or minor, find out what the specific pre-requisites are for that field.

★ **Writing classes**. Most colleges require all freshmen students to take a writing course, which teaches students how to research, develop and write a paper. Many students see this either as a bore, an easy A grade or both, but there is usually such a wide variety of classes to choose from you should be able to find something to interest you. Few students are allowed to place out of this class.

★ **Physical Education**. This may also be a requirement to graduate, but there is almost always a large variety and fun array of classes on offer.

★ **MOOCs** – Massive Open Online Courses. More and more colleges are offering these online and distance learning courses and some give credit for them. However, according to the US Government's *Study in the States* web site, as an F1 student you may only count one online course (equivalent to three credits) toward your course-load of study per semester or term. English language program students may *not* count MOOCs toward a full course of study. If you have questions, you are advised to contact your college's DSO or e-mail the appropriate official at – sevp@ice.dhs.gov.

★ **Week-day spread**. Most classes occur several times per week and you'll have a couple of different options – Monday, Tuesday and Friday mornings, or Monday Wednesday and Thursday afternoons. This gives you the chance to spread your classes and your homework load evenly throughout the week. It may seem like a great idea to have few or no classes on Fridays and Mondays, but that means your workload (including homework) is crammed into the middle of the week.

⚠ **WARNING**
Although a class might be offered at different times during the week, they are not always taught by the same professor. If you have a preference for a specific professor make sure you have registered for the days when he or she is scheduled to teach.

★ **Early bird or night owl**. Similarly, you may have the choice of morning or afternoon classes. If you're an early bird, schedule the early classes. If you choose later classes, consider other issues such as getting to and from your dorm on dark winter evenings.

★ **Location of classes**. This might seem trivial but giving yourself 15 minutes between two classes and then discovering you'll need to get the campus bus between them will obviously cause problems. There will be a campus map on the web site and each class you're considering will have a location listed. If in doubt go to the student forum or Facebook page and ask for advice. If you have already been allocated an advisor, s/ he can also help.

> ⚠ **WARNING**
> Many professors include attendance and punctuality when grading, and have a deadline of 10 or 15 minutes, after which you will be marked as having skipped the class.

★ **Degree of difficulty**. Although you can read student blogs to get an idea of how difficult certain classes are (either intellectually challenging or a crippling work load), you won't really know until you start the class and see for yourself. Try to give yourself a mix of classes with regard to difficulty, at least until you know what you can handle. Certain classes, such as English Literature, involve a lot of reading so make sure you schedule plenty of time for that. You're also more likely to get good grades if you study subjects you enjoy. Your pre-requisites or 'Gen Ed' classes will ensure you have at least a few that aren't to your liking!

★ **Reading load**. If English isn't your first language, remember required reading will probably take you a lot longer than reading in your own language. Don't sign up for too many classes with a large reading requirement.

★ **Successful registration**. When registering for classes online, you will know immediately whether you're successful or not. As a freshman you might not get all the classes you want, as more senior students may have enrolled already. Don't worry or panic, just keep checking back. Some students over-enroll with a view to changing their schedule at a later date, therefore vacancies often arise. Remember many classes are offered continuously so you may be able to take it the following semester.

★ **Drop/ Add**. The first few weeks of the semester will be a 'drop/ add' period where you can drop a class and register for another, depending on availability and whether or not it fits in with the rest of your classes. In many cases you will need approval from your academic advisor and/ or the class professors involved. Do not stop turning up for class as this will be considered an incomplete or an unauthorized withdrawal, which, in many colleges, is the equivalent of failing a class. Failing a class has a negative impact on your college GPA.

⚠ **WARNING**
Check with the International Students Office if you drop a class without taking another in its place, as you may have inadvertently fallen out of visa status.

★ **Class codes**. All classes in the catalog are numbered, so make sure you key in the correct numbers. Typically, classes beginning with the number 1 are introductory or general level classes – classes beginning with a 2 are usually intermediate and for upper level students. If taking classes above the first level, check to see whether you need permission from the professor.

Books

Once you know you've been accepted in a certain class, you can think about buying the books you'll need. Be aware the price of books sometimes goes up as you near the start of the semester:

★ **Online purchase**. When you register for classes, your college web site may automatically inform you which books are required for each class and take you to an online site where you can purchase them. Alternatively your college bookstore may have information regarding books for all classes.

★ **Are all books necessary?** If it's possible try to find out whether all of the books on a particular class list are required. Occasionally professors list books that are optional. If some books are required, but won't be used very much, they may be a rental option.

★ **Online book orders collected at college**. If you can register for classes prior to coming to the US, you can probably order your books online and they will be boxed and ready for you when you arrive at college. It may pay to wait until nearer the time semester starts for a few reasons. You might change your mind about the classes you've registered for and, more importantly, the professor may change the list of texts right before classes start. (Ask about this on the college student forum or on the Facebook page.) If you arrive at college a week or two before classes start, that's usually enough time to walk in and get your books or order them, and the bookstore staff can assist you – although leaving it till the last minute may cost you more.

★ **Book rental**. Some colleges have a system which allows you to rent books instead of purchasing them. This is a great option when you'll only need books for one semester. You'll also find students looking to sell textbooks, which is a great option as long as you know the book is still on the list for your class. Your college may also quote you the new and used prices for books.

★ **Searching online bookstores**. You can search the many online bookstores for cheaper books. Make sure you type in the correct title, edition and ISBN (International Standard Book Number) as you may have to pay to return incorrect books. Also check the shipping information to ensure the book will reach you before classes start. Remember to factor the shipping costs into the cost when shopping online.

★ Online options for book rental. In addition to your college book store there are many online options for renting books:
  - www.text-bookrentals.com
  - www.campusbookrentals.com
  - www.chegg.com
  - www.collegebookrenter.com
  - www.amazon.com – Amazon also has discounted student rates, see web site for details
  - www.barnesandnoble.com
  - www.ecampus.com
  - www.bookrenter.com

★ Comparing college bookstore against Internet options. It is worth comparing prices against your college bookstore and against a few Internet sites. Consider the following:
  - Prices
  - Price-matching policies
  - Rental periods
  - Late fees and fines
  - Shipping and return prices
  - Shipping options
  - Rental extension possibilities
  - Whether you can highlight in the book
  - What condition the book must be returned in
  - If you get discounts for referring friends to the site
  - Whether you can buy the book after the rental period

★ **College Library**. Other options, especially if you'll only need a book for one semester, is to see if the college library allows you to borrow books for the duration or to consider down-loading a book if your professor allows it.

★ **Rental books and online homework**. If you decide not to buy new, make sure your professor isn't listing a book that has an online access code for homework. If you buy or rent a used book you might have to pay more for the online access.

Bedding and other dorm room basics

College dorm rooms are typically very basic and bare and you'll need to provide many items yourself. Obviously if you're flying halfway round the world, you probably won't be bringing everything with you. Besides, it's often cheaper to buy stuff once you're in the USA. The information from your college will usually include a 'what you'll need' list of items for your dorm room, which will include everything from pillows and bedding, to trash cans, mirrors and notice-boards. It will also include a list of prohibited items you should pay attention to.

There are a few companies who sell a set of everything you'll need at what looks like a really low price. The quality of the merchandise is sometimes questionable as I found out a few years ago. Before my daughter's freshman year I ordered a complete bed and bath set – the sheets dyed her skin blue overnight, the towels were almost too prickly to use and the duvet/ comforter filling migrated to one end before the semester was halfway through. Not a good bargain!

Although they say they can ship items to you, some of these companies don't ship to college dorms and will assume you have a home address in the States. This is the time to use the incoming freshmen Facebook page, or other student blogs, as they can tell you how easy it is to buy bedding and other items in the vicinity of your college.

Bed, Bath and Beyond, JC Penney and Target are national chains in the States offering decent quality merchandise and shipping to college dorms and there are dozens more who do this. When ordering and shipping bedding, note:

★ The beds will probably be 'twin' (i.e. single) but are usually 'extra long' so make sure you're ordering sheets that match the bed size.

★ The shipping address probably won't be the same as your dorm address (i.e. there will probably be a specific mailroom address).

Look out for college-organized trips to local stores and for sales around the time of classes starting. You can often buy basics for your room at greatly reduced prices. Sometimes it pays to wait until you see what you need in your room, and to wait for the big sales.

⚠ **WARNING**

It may not be worth bringing electronic items to the USA if the voltage is different. American appliances are 120 volts (60Hz) and have specific plugs and wall outlets. You can buy converters for foreign appliances, but it might be cheaper to buy the American appliance once you arrive on campus.

Here is a great web site for checking to see if your country is compatible – http://users.telenet.be/worldstandards/electricity.htm#voltage_table.

Computers

Most colleges offer discounts on computers and printers at their campus stores. If you don't already own a laptop or desktop, or are considering up-grading, make sure to check your college web site first. As well as offering discounted prices many colleges offer minor repairs free of charge if you buy your laptop from them. Other considerations are:

★ **Laptop or desktop?** In most cases, a laptop is more practical as it's portable. Given most campuses have free Wi-Fi, you'll probably be moving around with your computer.

★ **Software options**. Your choice of computer may be dictated by the applications and software used on campus. If you have been accepted into a specific school or department, check their web page to look for their software requirements too.

★ **Security**. Purchase a cable lock if you buy a laptop. They will be sold at the college store and other computer stores, and allow you to secure your laptop wherever you are working. The cable wraps around the laptop and can be attached to any solid, stable fixture. Most dorm room desks have an opening or hole through which to thread the cable.

★ **Printer?** Sometimes, when you buy a new computer, you get the printer free. If you decide to purchase a printer wait until you have seen your dorm room and know what size would fit. Most colleges have printing available to students either in the computer center or at the library. Although this may seem expensive per page, you may already have been charged for it in your semester fees. Many professors accept electronic submission of documents, so you might find you don't need your own printer very often. Don't forget to research the cost of replacement ink cartridges, which can be extremely high.

★ **Technology**. Most college web sites have a dedicated page for Technology, as well as a phone number to call if you have problems.

Cell/ mobile phones

Called cell phones in the USA, there are many options of models and calling plans to choose from and most phone companies run special promotions throughout the year. As the plans on offer change frequently it's not possible to give up-to-the-minute information here:

★ **Phone companies**. The largest national phone companies in the US are AT&T, Comcast, Sprint, T-Mobile, US Cellular, and Verizon. There are a number of regional carriers offering cell phone plans too.

★ **Calling plans**. If you need to purchase a phone or calling plan, your first step is to check your college web site. Some colleges have deals with specific phone carriers and may be able to get lower rates for students, cheaper phones or no-cost repairs.

★ **Coverage**. You should find out what the coverage is like at your campus for the various cell phone providers. Phone company web sites have a coverage map showing where their 3G and 4G coverage is strong. As some areas and buildings report bad reception, do your research to make sure you don't choose a company that typically drops calls on campus. College chat rooms and forums are a great place to obtain this information.

★ **Free Wi-Fi?** Check to see if there is free Wi-Fi on campus and whether it's available everywhere or only in certain spots such as libraries. (Most American colleges have high-speed Internet access in dorm rooms, as well as free Wi-Fi.)

★ **Phone compatibility**. Not all phones are compatible with every provider, so don't buy a phone until you've decided on the plan you need. If you already have a phone, your choices may be limited.

★ **Cell phone plans**. Cell phone providers offer Post-paid plans and Pre-paid plans (or Pay-As-You-Go plans). For a variety of prices these plans cover phone calls, text messaging and Internet data retrieval. Many web sites ask for the zip code where the phone will be used most, so make sure you have your college's zip code to hand when researching this – the zip code is part of the college's mailing address and can usually be found at the foot of the college home page, or under the 'Contact' details:

- **Contract phones**. Post-paid plans usually involve a one or two-year contract, and you'll pay a set monthly fee for your phone (and data) usage. There is typically a fee of $100 and more for early termination of this contract. Users must usually demonstrate a good personal credit history, which is difficult for many college students. In addition there may be a deposit to pay as well as set-up costs, although the monthly plans are generally the best price and a free phone is often included.

- **Pay-as-you-go plans**. Pre-paid plans or pay-as-you-go plans require no contract, no credit check and no commitment. You choose a plan giving you a specific amount of minutes per month and you can purchase refill cards or top up your account with a credit card. Different phone companies attach various deals to these refill cards, such as lower price per minute with a minimum $100 refill. Typically if you want texts and data on the plan, you have to add them separately.

★ **Pre-paid phones**. If you don't already own a phone you can buy one with a pre-paid plan already installed. Most of the large phone companies now offer something, as do giant retailers such as Target and Walmart.

★ **Pre-paid SIM cards**. Many phone companies and retailers offer pre-paid SIM cards you can use on your existing phone if it is an unlocked GSM cell phone. An Internet search will bring up many options and rates. In general a pre-paid SIM card will give you a US telephone number and requires no credit checking or long-term commitment. Check with your phone manufacturer to find out whether your phone will work in the USA and pay attention to the phone networks the SIM card will work with. Check the network is reliable in your college's area.

★ **Minutes and international calls**. Other considerations should include whether or not you can carry unused minutes over into the next month, and what the international rates are if you're going to be calling home on that phone. Make sure you know if you are being charged for incoming, as well as out-going calls, as many phone companies do this.

> ⚠ **WARNING**
>
> Many US phone companies charge astronomical rates for calling when you go outside of the USA. While your international calling rate (i.e. calling home) might seem reasonable, using your American phone in your home country won't be at the same rate. Talk to your phone provider before traveling outside the US and make sure you're not going to get hit with hundreds of dollars in calling, texting and data retrieval charges. There are additional and temporary plans you can add on when traveling, and with data retrieval remember to turn off 'data roaming' or purchase a plan to cover you (or don't download from the Internet on your phone).

★ Free Text messaging. Look for free international text messaging services such as WhatsApp – www.whatsapp.com. '*WhatsApp Messenger is a cross-platform mobile messaging app which allows you to exchange messages without having to pay for SMS. WhatsApp Messenger is available for iPhone, BlackBerry, Android, Windows Phone and Nokia and yes, those phones can all message each other! Because WhatsApp Messenger uses the same internet data plan that you use for e-mail and web browsing, there is no cost to message and stay in touch with your friends.'*

📖 FURTHER READING

For more information, see Kiplinger's advice –
www.kiplinger.com/magazine/archives/smart-ways-to-save-
on-smartphone-plans.html

Mail-box

In order to receive mail through the United States Postal Service, students are required to have an official US PO Box. Mail is not usually delivered directly to your dorm room. Some colleges automatically allocate freshmen or all students a mail-box and others direct you to the USPS web site where you must apply for a PO Box and set it up yourself – there will be specific instructions about this on your freshmen web pages.

When you arrive on campus you will have to register and collect your key or code for the mail-box. There is an annual fee which is outlined on the USPS web site, but your college may give a discount or include this in its billing.

✔ TIP

Packages delivered through services such as Federal Express and DHL are not delivered to your PO Box, but usually to the campus mailroom, which might have a different mailing address. Make sure you give this address to anyone who might send you a parcel or package.

Travel plans

With an F1 student visa, you may arrive in the USA 30 days prior to your college start date, which is registered in the SEVIS system by the college. You must register with your school on or before the start date or you will not be *maintaining your status* and could be deported before you start studying. See next chapter for what you will need to gain entry to the USA and don't forget to visit the US Immigration web sites to keep up to date with any changes. Your ISO will probably send out e-mails alerting you to any changes in laws or procedures so don't ignore them.

Your plans should include how you are going to travel from the airport or border, to your campus. Some colleges will organize transportation or have shuttle buses, but many won't. Unless you have specifically discussed it don't assume there will be someone there to meet you, or that there will be any form of public transport between the two locations.

FURTHER READING
The government's web site, Study in the States, gives up-to-date information on travel requirements and many other aspects of being a foreign student in the USA.
http://studyinthestates.dhs.gov/2013/04/summer-break-travel-reminder

Chapter Nine
On Arrival

On your arrival in the USA, you will first encounter government officials who will check your paperwork and luggage to make sure everything is in order. A Non-Immigrant visa in your passport doesn't automatically grant you entry. You may also have biometric information taken from you (fingerprints or a photo) for future identity verification. This chapter covers the government procedures you will encounter on arrival and the college requirements after that.

Customs and Immigration

According to the Customs and Border Protection web site – http://www.cbp.gov/xp/cgov/travel/id_visa/ you should have the following documents on your person **not** in your checked luggage (if you are flying):

★ A valid passport including attached envelope of immigration documents
★ **Original** SEVIS Form I-20AB, I-20MN, or DS-2019
★ Form I-797, Receipt Notice or Internet Receipt verifying SEVIS fee payment
★ Evidence of financial resources consistent with your I-20 form

📖 **FURTHER READING**
For additional SEVP/ SEVIS Program Information refer to
the US Immigration and Customs Enforcement web site –
http://www.ice.gov/sevis/students/index.htm.
The government's Study in the States web site also gives
excellent information on what to expect when you enter
the USA – http://studyinthestates.dhs.gov/2013/04/here-to-
help-what-to-expect-at-a-port-of-entry-with-a-u-s-customs-
and-border-protection-officer.

In addition, it is recommended you carry the following:

★ Evidence of Student/ Exchange Visitor status (recent tuition
receipts, transcripts)
★ Name and contact information for Designated School Official
(DSO) or Responsible Officer (RO) at your intended school or
program – if you are arriving outside of regular business hours
make sure you have a way to contact this person
★ Writing instrument (pen)

When you have your passport and visa checked at Immigration,
the government official may engage you in conversation and ask
questions about your reasons for coming to the USA. Don't panic
– they do this with lots of people and it doesn't automatically mean
there's a problem:

★ On the flight or at the border you will receive a customs form (CF
6059) which you should complete and present when requested.
Don't lose any of your paperwork or copies thereof. The I-94
Arrivals/ Departures information is now taken from your passport
and stored electronically at the time of arrival. A paper I-94 is
only issued when entering the USA by land or under special
circumstances. Travel documents are stamped with date and class
of entry, and duration of your permitted stay. You can access/ print

off your I-94 information at www.cbp.gov/I94. The website also has a factsheet explaining the new procedures.

★ Once you have cleared Customs and Immigration you should have a plan for getting to your college. Don't assume there will be someone there to meet you or that there will be public transportation. It is important to plan this in advance as a cab ride to a campus fifty miles away could pose a real problem.

★ Government regulations require you to register your presence at your college by completing international student check-in procedures – your college will give you directions to this check-in, which is often an orientation session.

★ You need the precise address of where to report when you first arrive on campus. Some college campuses are huge and being dropped off at the wrong location with several suitcases isn't funny. Passing students won't necessarily know where your orientation is, so make sure you know whether you're supposed to report to a dorm, the International Students Office, the Student Building or another location.

International student check-in/ orientation

Try to arrive a day or two before orientation to combat jet lag and get yourself settled. If you were assigned *pre-orientation homework* make sure this is completed as registration for classes may depend on it:

 WARNING
Your SEVIS document will contain the latest date you can enter the USA and register with your college. It is very important not to miss this deadline as you may be denied entry if you do.

★ As international orientation is typically before regular classes start, your campus housing may not be available to you. If this is the case your college will have given you information about nearby hotels, and it is important to have somewhere booked before you arrive. If you are able to check-in to what will be your regular dorm room, there may be an additional daily fee to pay.

★ At check-in or orientation you will complete your student arrival information online and receive information about your Non-Immigrant status. If you already have a job on campus you will probably begin your application for a Social Security number too. If you haven't already sent them ahead, your immunization records will be requested at this point. In short, make sure you have all your official paperwork with you when you check-in.

★ Your orientation session may include registration for classes. Please see the previous chapter for detailed information about registration. The registration deadline for F1 students is 30 days after classes begin otherwise your SEVIS record is terminated and you will be out of *legal status*.

✔ **TIP**

If you are attending an international students' orientation just before classes start, look at the schedule carefully. As Columbian student Juliana Tamayo discovered, "The international orientation was in August, which I found a little inconvenient because it was at the same time as move-in day – most of the international students missed out on important time to buy items they needed and to get to know the city and dorms." Build in time to shop for whatever you need if you can.

Campus to-do list

Once you have all the official matters taken care of, there are many campus related things to do. There will probably be welcome events all over campus and an army of helpful student volunteers who can point you in the right direction for everything you need to do:

★ **Contact number**. Give your parents or family members a contact telephone number other than your cell phone. This can be the International Students Office, your Dorm Room assistant or your academic advisor, but they should always have a landline to contact in emergencies.

★ **Pick up your student ID and/ or dining cards**. This is one of the first things you'll need to do. The college ID card will give you access to most university buildings such as the library, gym, computer center and even your own residence hall. In some colleges this card is also your dining card. For some students your card will be given out at orientation, and others will have to line up at one of the campus administration buildings:

- In most cases you will need a photo ID and your college web site user name/ log in information to pick up your ID card.
- If you were required to send a digital photo for the card, and failed to do so, there probably won't be a card waiting for you and you'll need to speak to someone in the ID office.
- You will need to carry your ID card at all times – if the college is offering lanyards grab one of those too (a lanyard is a cord worn around the neck to which you can attach your ID cards) – if you don't want to wear a lanyard, choose a safe place for you ID card where it won't get bent or destroyed.
- Most colleges have a web site page devoted to ID matters – this is an obvious place to go with any questions you have.
- Many colleges have nicknames for their ID card – pay attention when reading about them, examples include the Cougar card at the University of Houston, the Raider card at Texas Tech and the GO card at Georgetown.

TIP
If you arrive before the majority of students collect your ID card as soon as you can to avoid the long lines ('queues').

★ **Walk your classes.** When you registered for classes you should have checked the location of each class, the distance between it and the next classroom, and the time you have to get from A to B. Even so, you should take the time to walk to each location before your first class and familiarize yourself with the routes between classes. Many professors take attendance and being more than 5-15 minutes late makes you a 'no show'. Depending on the professor or the college policy this could have severe consequences. In many cases attendance at the first class is confirmation of enrolment in that class – not being able to find the class will not be deemed a legitimate excuse for being late.

★ **Campus buildings.** Although your orientation program probably introduced you to the most important buildings on campus, it's a good idea to stroll around at your own pace and re-acquaint yourself with the layout. Find the cafeterias, library, mailroom, student center, other dorms, the International Students Office and the medical center. Most campuses name their buildings after dignitaries, donors and emeritus professors rather than calling them by their function, so it may take a while to remember them all.

★ **Mail-box.** If you applied for a US PO Box prior to your arrival (see previous chapter), you must register and pick up your key or code from the appropriate mail office on campus. Some colleges now allow you to retrieve a mail number online, which is used to access your mail-box. Mail is not normally delivered to individual dorm rooms, so without an official US PO Box your mail might be returned to the sender. In some colleges incoming freshmen are automatically allocated a mail-box, but you'll still have to register and pick up your key on arrival.

★ **Pick up or purchase your books**. If you ordered your books online from your college they will generally be waiting for pickup at the college bookstore. Remember to take your college ID and the paper receipt or order confirmation.

★ **Go shopping**. Many colleges have an excursion for students to a local mega-store where you will be able to buy anything and everything for your dorm room. Transportation is usually free and you may need to sign up, but this is a good idea as these stores can be miles from campus and difficult to get to even by public transportation. Look for signs around campus or ask at your Welcome Center/ Student Building.

★ **Get a state ID**. Most Americans use a driving license as their main form of photo ID but this is not always possible for F1 students. You will be able to obtain a state ID for identity purposes, and this can be used instead of carrying your passport around:
- State ID cards are issued by your state's DMV (Department of Motor Vehicles). You can find your state web information at the main DMV web site – www.dmv.org. Documentation requirements are specific to each state so you should check before applying. There is also a government fact sheet at – www.ice.gov/doclib/sevis/pdf/dmv_factsheet.pdf.

★ **Finding a job**. If you planned to work while at college now's the time to start looking:
- Freshmen holding F1 visas are allowed to work up to 20 hours per week on campus and 40 hours during the summer and college breaks.
- You are not authorized to work off campus, so make sure the job you find doesn't put you out of visa status. Amanda Ecklar, of Yale University's Office for International Students and Scholars, finds, "… because so many American students have off-campus jobs, international students often fail to appreciate that such a job would immediately put them at risk for deportation.

International students are not eligible for work-study positions on campus as these are funded by the US government and are for US citizens." Before being eligible for Curricular Practical Training (CPT) or Optional Practical Training (OPT) you must be in your program of study for one academic year.

- Most colleges have a few paid positions available, ranging from tutoring, to cafeteria work, fund-raising and lab assisting – there is normally a student-oriented page on the college web site listing all campus positions currently open, and many colleges hold job fares or seminars to help you.

- When you secure a job you must get authorization from your DSO before you begin working – if you don't have work eligibility paperwork filed you are out of visa status – check with your International Students Office for specific instructions.

★ **Volunteering**. You will find many American students volunteer in various charitable organizations either on campus or in the local town or city. As an F1 student you may volunteer as long as you don't receive any taxable income from it. In addition, if the position is one for which an employer would ordinarily hire someone, you must obtain work authorization from your DSO and apply for a Social Security number. In such cases you will be limited to 20 hours per week. Go to – www.serve.gov to find volunteer opportunities in your area and see the government web site for more information – http://studyinthestates.dhs.gov/2011/10/may-i-volunteer-while-studying-in-the-states.

★ **Sign up**. Sign up for clubs, teams and organizations, but don't overdo it. Many college freshmen are a little overwhelmed at the amount of reading required for core courses. While it's a good strategy to sign up for a few extra-curricular activities, make sure you're not overcommitting yourself until you know what your course-load will be. Try to choose a few activities that allow you to drop out or decrease your involvement if need be.

Most colleges have hundreds of clubs and organizations to choose from, with interests ranging from chess to Quidditch and beyond. If you can't find anything that suits, you can often start your own club, as long as you go through the right channels. Many colleges are even able to offer funding to new organizations. Some of the more academic organizations may have a GPA or specialization requirement for membership.

There will typically be a fair, bazaar or other large event where most of the college organizations set up a booth and compete for your attention. You will see posters all over campus advertising various activities and clubs. Your college web site will also have a list of activities as they usually require them to be registered and approved.

★ **Pledging**. Most colleges have fraternities and sororities. These are large, mainly social organizations named as Greek letters, to which you must be invited to join (pledge). Some fraternities and sororities operate at a national and international level. There are also Professional, Service and Honors fraternities, which have different rules regarding eligibility and membership. Colleges with social fraternities and sororities will have a PanHellenic Council to govern all Greek activities on campus. Some colleges have high student participation in Greek life, and in other colleges Greek participation will be under 25%. This percentage will give you an indication of how social activities are organized on campus. If most students pledge and you don't, you might find yourself excluded from a lot of socializing as many events will be limited to members only:
- **Rush Week**. At the beginning of the fall semester most Greek organizations recruit new members. This is generally referred to as Rush Week, and individuals looking into or applying to fraternities/ sororities are said to be *rushing*. In some colleges this is a very intense, competitive period, full of anxiety as to which (usually) sorority a student can get into, and in others it's very laid

back. If you are at all unsure about *rushing* or *pledging* wait until your sophomore year – that way you can spend a year learning about Greek life on your campus and make an informed decision.

- **Registration fees**. Most Greek organizations require members to pay registration fees as well as annual fees, so that's something to think about when making a decision. They often specify a minimum GPA in order to become a member. If your high school academic record doesn't translate into a GPA this should not automatically preclude you from Greek Life.

- **Formal recognition of Greek life**. Fraternities and sororities do not have to be formally recognized at their colleges, although most are. Interestingly, Princeton does not recognize any such organization, there is no frat/ sorority housing and, as of the fall 2012 semester, freshmen will not be allowed to engage in any form of Greek life, including Rush Week. An increasing number of colleges (currently mostly Ivy League) are introducing *delayed-Rush policies*, whereby students are not permitted to pledge until the second half of freshman year or the beginning of sophomore year.

- **Recruitment and membership**. Some college organizations take pledging very seriously, with rules, manuals and sanctions covering the various stages of rushing, bidding and pledging. Where there is a lot of competition for membership, recruitment tends to be very formalized and resembles a week-long speed-dating event. *Rushees* visit a series of Open Houses and parties held by the various frats or sororities in which they are interested. There begins a process of 'mutual selection', which means while you are required to declare your preferences, you can also be 'cut' from their list of desirable pledges, i.e. you might like them but they don't want you.

- **Greek life at different colleges**. For more information on sorority life visit – www.TheSororityLife.com. Also visit a few college web sites to get an idea of how the whole system works at various degrees of seriousness. The following college web sites give clear information on Greek life on their campuses:

▷ University of Pennsylvania (UPenn) –
   http://www.upennpanhellenic.org/sorority-recruitment
▷ The University of Mississippi ('Ole Miss') –
   http://dos.orgsync.com/Recruitment

★ Get out and meet people. Rendy Schrader, Director of International Student and Scholar Advising, Indiana University, advises all international students to, "… get out there and get involved on campus as soon as they arrive." The students you'll meet in your first semester will probably be good friends throughout college, if not for life. Staying in your room or studying full-time in the library may get you a high GPA, but it can mean you don't bond with other students for a while. Before you know it, tight friendships are formed and you're not part of things. Although it may sound excruciating, if someone has their dorm room open, knock and introduce yourself – if you want people to do the same, leave your door open and say 'Hi' as they walk by. Most people are in the same boat and everyone is looking to make friends.

Chapter Ten
US College life - The Lowdown

There's no doubt you've cleared the biggest hurdle by getting into an American college. If your previous education was nothing like the American system, you will have a lot of new things coming at you in the first few months. Even if you are familiar with the American system, if you've never lived in the USA before there's still a lot to learn. This chapter will cover the basics of American college life and give you the vocabulary you'll need to get by. It does not cover detailed information beyond your first semester as you will learn most of that by being at college.

Official rules and regulations

You need to stay on the right track in order to keep your F1 status and your college place, so it's important to know the official rules and regulations.

Visa status

Having a visa in your passport is not the same as *maintaining visa status*. The visa is for travel purposes and allows you to enter and re-enter the USA. To maintain status, your I-20, I-94 and passport must all be current and it is your responsibility to make sure you are in compliance at all times. Your college will have a DSO (Designated School Official) to help you do this but he or she is not authorized to issue visas.

Government regulations regarding visas change frequently and it's up to you to keep abreast of all changes. Your International Students Office will send out regular e-mails about such changes, so be sure to read them:

 TIP

Status is pronounced with a flat 'a' in the USA, *stat–us* as opposed to the British sounding *stay-tus*.

★ **First day of classes**. Your I-20 will show the date on which you are expected to begin classes at college. Failure to enroll by the specified date will render you *out of status*. If there are any changes in residence, study program, employment or college, they must be authorized by the DSO and submitted to SEVIS within 10 days.

★ **Full time enrollment**. To maintain visa status you must be enrolled as a full-time student at all times, at the college specified on your I-20. Make sure you are meeting the minimum number of credit hours your college requires for full time enrollment. You are considered *in status* during your college's annual/ summer break.

★ **Academic and disciplinary standing**. If you are subject to academic or disciplinary sanctions at your college this could result in the loss of your I-20, which will usually mean deportation from the US at your own expense.

★ **Employment.** As a freshman F1 Non-Immigrant, you are allowed to work 20 hours on campus and 40 hours during semester/ term breaks. Any unauthorized employment is not allowed on your particular visa and could result in the loss of that visa. *Unauthorized* means your employer is someone other than the college or organization that provides service to the college. Make sure you obtain authorization to hold the position of employment in question, as detailed in *Chapter Nine – On Arrival.*

★ **Completion of studies.** After completion of studies international students are allowed 60 days to organize their departure from the USA. If you obtain authorization to withdraw early, you will have 15 days to depart.

★ **Withdrawal.** If you withdraw from your study program for any reason, you must leave the USA even if your I-20 is still valid.

📖 **FURTHER READING**
See the US government web site for up-to-date information on maintaining F1 visa status –
http://travel.state.gov/visa/temp/types/types_1268.html#13

★ **Extending your stay.** If you wish to extend your stay beyond the expiry of your F1 visa, you must apply to the US Citizenship and Immigration Services (USCIS) before the expiration date. Staying on an expired visa risks deportation and being barred from re-entry to the USA in the future.

★ **Expired passport.** If your passport expires, but the visa is still valid, you should travel with your old passport and visa in addition to your new passport.

★ **Expiration of visa**. If your F1 visa expires but you are still *in status* (i.e. your I-20, I-94 and passport are valid) you can stay in the USA. As your visa is for travel purposes, you will need to renew it for re-entry into the country.

★ **Travel signatures**. While anyone can leave the USA international students need certain paperwork for re-entry. If your absence from the USA is for less than five months, in addition to your passport, your F1 visa, your I-94 and your I-20 form, you must request a travel signature (official endorsement) from your college **BEFORE** you depart. (See page 3 of your I-20 document.) This endorsement states you are in good standing with your college and eligible for re-entry, and is valid for one year.

 WARNING

Unless your country has an exemption agreement with the USA, your passport must be valid for at least six months after the date of re-entry. There is a long list of exempt countries on the government web site, as well as detailed instructions for F1 re-entry –
http://www.ice.gov/sevis/travel/faq_f2.htm#_Toc81222004

The travel signature is required for any overseas visit including trips back home. If you are planning to travel to any other country outside of the USA, check with that country's embassy or consulate to see if you require an entry visa. If, for any reason, you leave for longer than five months, you will need a new I-20 from your college to re-enter the USA.

A travel signature is typically obtained from the International Students Office and must only be given by a DSO (Designated School Official.)

Tax returns

All international students and their dependents are required to file a US Federal Tax Return each year, whether or not they have earned any US-sourced income – http://www.irs.ustreas.gov/pub/irs-pdf/f8843.pdf. You may also be required to file state and city tax returns.

 TIP
The requirement to file does not mean you will owe money in taxes.

The annual deadline will be mid-April or mid-June depending on your income and tax status, and all returns filed must be date-stamped by that deadline. There is no cost to submit a tax return to the IRS (Internal Revenue Service), although tax advice from a relevant professional probably won't be free. At present the IRS does not allow foreign students to file electronically:

★ **Tax forms**. The International Students Office may be able to advise you about forms relevant to your situation and how to file them, but these staff members are not tax experts. In most cases they will provide software and tax seminars at least once a year, to help international students understand the requirements and the process. Filing a tax return in the USA can be a complicated business so you are advised to sign up and attend tax seminars.

★ **Scholarships and tax**. According to the IRS, in some cases Nonresident Aliens must pay Federal Income tax on scholarships if that grant is from an American institution or individual – http://www.irs.gov/businesses/small/international/article/0,,id=96431,00.html.

In addition: '*In general, the taxable portion of a scholarship or fellowship paid to a NONRESIDENT ALIEN is subject to Federal income tax withholding at the rate of 30%, unless the payments are exempt from tax under the Internal Revenue Code or a tax treaty. However, payees who are temporarily present in the United States in F-1, J-1, M-1, Q-1, or Q-2 nonimmigrant status are subject to a reduced 14% withholding rate on the taxable portion of the grant because such individuals are considered to be engaged in a U.S. trade or business under Internal Revenue Code section 871(c).*

Students only: In general, those portions of a scholarship, fellowship, or grant used to pay tuition, fees, books, supplies, or equipment are classified as a "Qualified Scholarship" and are not includible in the gross income of the recipient under Internal Revenue Code section 117 if the recipient is a candidate for a degree. Any portion of the scholarship, fellowship, or grant that does not correlate to the five items mentioned above is includible in the gross income of the recipient, which means that it is subject to withholding.'

Exceptions exist where the US and your home country have a tax treaty or where there are exceptions under the Internal Revenue Code.

⚠ **WARNING**
Please note this is not tax advice. Tax can be a complicated affair and you are advised to go to your International Students Office in the first instance and to seek professional tax advice and assistance.

★ **Social Security and Medicare taxes**. '*F-visas, J-visas, M-visas, Q-visas. Nonresident Alien students, scholars, professors, teachers, trainees, researchers, physicians, au pairs, summer camp workers, and other aliens temporarily present in the United States in F-1,J-1,M-1, or Q-1/Q-2 nonimmigrant status are exempt on wages paid* *to them for services performed within the United States as long as such services are allowed by USCIS for these nonimmigrant statuses, and such services are performed to carry out the purposes for which such visas were issued to them.'* (IRS)

★ **Seek tax advice before you file**. Do not try to file your own taxes without first seeking assistance and information. Such information and/ or tax advice will help you with the following:
  - Residency status
  - Type of payment
  - Expenses information
  - The correct form(s) to submit
  - Attachments to include
  - Relevant deadlines
  - Possible tax treaty with your country
  - State and city tax liability

★ **Before filing**. Before you file, make copies of everything and keep them in a safe place where there is no risk of the information being copied. If you are financially sponsored in any way, speak to your program sponsor before beginning the filing process, as they may have to be involved. You are advised to keep copies of your tax filings for a minimum of six years as the government can audit individuals that far back if substantial errors are discovered.

★ The IRS does not send unsolicited e-mails or faxes regarding tax refunds or asking for personal or financial information. If you receive either, they are part of a scam and you should not divulge any information to them.

📖 **FURTHER READING**
See the government web site for details –
http://www.irs.gov/businesses/small/international/
article/0,,id=96431,00.html

197

Social Security Number

To quote the government's web site: '*Social Security numbers generally are assigned to people who are authorized to work in the United States. Social Security numbers are used to report your wages to the government and to determine eligibility for Social Security benefits.*' In other words, if you are working on campus, you must apply for a Social Security number so your employer (the college) can make the necessary deductions – http://www.socialsecurity.gov/pubs/10181.html:

★ **Social Security Numbers**. As an international student the government recommends you wait at least 10 days after your arrival in the USA before applying for a Social Security number (SS#), and that you have registered with your college. This gives the Department of Homeland Security time to get your information into its system. It is best to apply before starting work, but it's not the end of the world if you can't. As soon as you get your Social Security card you should inform your employer. Your college DSO should be able to assist you with the Social Security administration.

★ **Identity Fraud**. Keep your Social Security number a closely guarded secret and don't lose your SS card. Anyone who gets hold of your SS information can use it to obtain credit in your name and cause untold damage – this is Identity Fraud. Although you will be asked for your SS number from authorized people, it is not advisable to carry your original card around with you and most people memorize their numbers. In general, work and bank related transactions will require your SS number. If anyone else asks for your number, ask why they need it and how it will be used. Many times it is being used as a means of personal identification and there may be another official document or number that would suffice, such as your college ID card.

★ **Security measures with SSN**. If your college routinely uses Social Security numbers for general ID, you may ask them to allocate a different number for the purpose. If there are any cards, paperwork or other items that display your Social Security number and are available to a wide audience, you should ask to have it removed. This includes your student ID card. Many colleges no longer use Social Security numbers as student ID data. If you lose your Social Security card or are worried about fraud, visit the government web site for instructions on how to report it.

Alcohol and Drug laws, policies and procedures

The age at which you can legally possess, purchase and/ or drink alcohol in the USA is 21. Whatever your college's policy is on the matter, and whatever your personal views, it is important to remember that disobeying the law can result in legal action being taken against you. As an international student a conviction would negatively impact your visa status and you would risk deportation. Even if you weren't convicted the college can still take disciplinary action against you, which would similarly jeopardize your visa status.

Although it is increasingly difficult to purchase alcohol as a minor, college students typically get round the ID barrier by having an older student buy it for them. It is illegal to drink or possess alcohol under 21, not only to purchase it. There are very severe penalties for using a false ID for the purpose of obtaining alcohol if you're underage.

Most college web sites have a policy statement on all aspects of student behavior, including those relating to drugs and alcohol. The policy usually covers alcohol and drug use on and off campus. You would be wise to glance over these pages earlier rather than later.

⚠️ **WARNING**

College policies differ regarding underage students caught with others who have been drinking. Some colleges treat it as if you had been drinking, even if only helping intoxicated friends. Make sure you know your college's policies.

State and county laws

In the USA many laws operate at the state and county level, therefore what may be true in California might not apply to someone in New Hampshire. Similarly, the consequences can vary widely too. While it is unrealistic to expect you to go through every law on the statute books, you should read anything that is linked on your college web site. These laws have been highlighted because they are relevant to student life in that state or county.

For example, in many 'dry' counties, where no alcohol is sold, the laws often go further than you'd imagine:

★ Southern Methodist University, which is situated in (dry) University Park in Dallas, reminds its students of the local law: '*In addition, transportation and/ or possession of more than 24 12-ounce bottles of beer or more than one quart of hard liquor, is considered prima facie evidence of intent to sell, and, therefore, evidence that the law has been violated. Alcoholic beverages that are transported into a dry area may not be transported back out of the dry area.*'

Campus police

Most colleges now have their own Police Department, and in many states campus police have full police powers and carry firearms. College campus police are there for your safety and also to keep you on the straight and narrow. Typically, their cars are not state or city police cars but carry the college insignia and identify themselves as campus police. They are often referred to as UPD – University Police Department.

College rules and regulations

As well as the US government regulations you must follow, your college will have its own policies and procedures governing student behavior.

Academic advisor

Before starting classes, you will have been assigned an academic advisor who you'll probably have for the full four years of your degree course. They are usually generalists, employed to advise across a wide spectrum of college matters and should be your first port of call. It makes sense to make yourself known to your academic advisor before you have a problem, so s/ he is better able to support and advise you when you do.

Academic integrity

College web sites all have detailed information covering what is acceptable and what is prohibited on campus. This covers both social and academic rules and you should make yourself familiar with all rules, as any infraction can have far-reaching consequences for international students:

★ **Plagiarism**. This is a serious offense and not taken lightly in the USA. With the increase in the use of Internet sources many college professors have tightened their rules on plagiarism, and you can still be disciplined and deported even if you didn't knowingly plagiarize.

   According to Amanda Eckler, of Yale University's Office for International Students and Scholars, "Problems often arise because of a student's lack of awareness or understanding of the matter; citations are a must. Plagiarism can get you kicked out of college." It is imperative you read the guidelines on your college's web site. If an individual professor or teaching assistant distributes guidelines in class, pay attention, as they are probably stricter than the general college policy.

   Plagiarism can mean anything from a short quotation without a citation, to large chunks of someone else's work being passed off as original work. Sanctions depend on the severity of the plagiarism and can entail a drop in grade, failing the class or being referred to the Dean for disciplinary measures. The latter may end up on file as a permanent academic record. I cannot stress how serious an offense this is, so please educate yourself on your college's position on it.

More and more educators are using anti-plagiarism software such as Turnitin to help detect unoriginal work. This software can detect work previously submitted by students themselves as well as work by others, and reaches several years into the past. In many cases your professor will immediately submit your electronic paper to one of these sites, which will generate a percentage of unoriginal content. If any of this percentage hasn't been credited to its original author, your paper will be sent off to the Dean's office with no further input from your professor. Fortunately most plagiarism checking web sites are accessible to students – find a reliable one (ask around, read reviews) and check your work before handing it in.

 WARNING
You can be guilty of plagiarizing yourself if you submit work previously written for another class. If you are taking two similar classes, avoid the risk of self-plagiarism by asking your professor how to handle this and how much repetition is acceptable. If your college offers a class or seminar on its plagiarism rules I strongly advise you to attend, as American rules are typically more stringent than elsewhere.

★ **Academic violations**. Other, equally serious, academic violations may include (and are not limited to) fabrication of data, dishonesty in online and classroom exams, inappropriate collaboration, and making threats or offering bribes with regard to your work or exams. Don't be tempted to allow someone else to take a test or write a paper for you and never agree to do this for another student.

★ **Disciplinary process**. Your college's web site will explain its disciplinary process as well as students' rights of appeal and all relevant deadlines. If you feel you are being sanctioned unfairly or incorrectly, make sure you deal with the problem immediately otherwise you may lose your right to appeal.

Class attendance

In most cases attendance at lectures, classes, labs etc., is a factor in determining your grades. Colleges will state a general policy and assign specific details to the individual professor. Obviously these details vary, but they should be clearly stated on the course syllabus, along with all other factors affecting your grade. Even in the event of minor illnesses such as a cold, many professors will not allow more than one or two absences from class per semester.

Excused absences are usually family and medical emergencies and college sports events (if you are a team member), so if you feel your absence falls into these categories you can argue your case. It is advisable to inform your professor before the absence and hope s/he allows you to make-up any test you miss or turn in work after the stated due date:

★ Should you need to take more than a few classes off because of an illness or family emergency, this is classed as a 'Leave of Absence' and you will most likely be required to make a formal request, as opposed to just taking time off.

Dorm rules

Your dorm or residence hall will have rules as to what you may or may not have in your room, as well as rules governing behavior of yourself and your guests. Infractions can result in you being asked to leave your residence. Banned items usually include candles, halogen lamps, toasters, pets, alcohol, illegal drugs, firearms and space heaters:

★ When you are assigned a dorm and a roommate, you may be asked to sign an agreement or contract with your roommate regarding acceptable and unacceptable behaviors. These discussions are meant to manage expectations and to avoid conflict and misunderstandings in the future. If your college or dorm doesn't require such an agreement, it is a good idea to have the conversation in the first few days of sharing. Areas to cover should include:
  - borrowing of personal items
  - whether overnight guests are allowed
  - lights out/ quiet time
  - cleanliness – who is responsible for what
  - prohibited items (alcohol/ drugs) in the room

★ If there are problems with your roommate or in the dorm, which can't be resolved by talking with the individual, you will have a Room Assistant on site, as well as Dorm Proctors and Presidents. They are there to ensure a smooth-running dorm and to assist students.

Drop/ add

As mentioned in *Chapter Eight – Before You Go – Visa Application and Other Important Steps*, there is a drop/ add period at the beginning of each semester where you may be able to change the classes you've registered for:

★ Except in exceptional circumstances classes may only be added or dropped during this specific period.

★ Adding or dropping some classes may require the written consent of a professor and/ or your academic advisor.

★ If you're trying to get into a class that is full, keep in touch with the professor without being a nuisance. Sometimes they are holding spots for juniors or seniors who need to take the class to fulfill graduation requirements. Once the professor establishes no more upper classmen are going to register, the class my open up to freshmen and sophomores.

★ International students are usually required to inform the International Students Office of changes to their class schedule.

★ After the drop/ add period if you decide, for any reason, that you don't want to continue with a particular class, don't stop attending. You are generally required to formally request a *Withdrawal* from the class from your professor. Rules differ from college to college, therefore your first conversation should be with your academic advisor or the class professor. An unauthorized withdrawal will result in a grade that is equivalent to a Fail, which will in turn negatively impact your GPA.

Hazing

Hazing is the practice of initiating college students (usually into fraternities and sororities and other organizations) by making them perform strenuous, embarrassing or dangerous tasks. Fortunately hazing is on the wane and is expressly forbidden at many colleges. The majority of states have some kind of law either criminalizing hazing, or requiring education establishments to have an anti-hazing program in place.

Do not submit to pressure to undergo an initiation that constitutes hazing. Your consent does not make the experience any less serious or criminal. If you are the victim of hazing contact someone in authority as soon as you can. Many colleges have hazing hotlines that can be found on the web site. If you are in serious physical or mental danger after being the victim of hazing, contact campus police.

No smoking rules

Your college might operate a smoke-free campus and your dorm will almost certainly ban smoking at all times. Your American peers will not hesitate to remind you of this rule should you choose to light up. Don't think you can smoke in a building without anyone finding out. If there is a duct system for air conditioning, the smoke will be sucked in and carried to other rooms. Additionally, the smoke may set off the dorm smoke alarms. You are expected to comply with no-smoking rules at all times and will be disciplined should you ignore the rules.

Academic information

As well as the official rules and regulations at your college, there will be general academic information you may not be familiar with.

Grading

Most colleges work on the 4.0 Grade Point Average system, although not all have the plus and minus elements seen below (4.0 is pronounced 'four-point-oh'). Exams and papers are often graded with marks out of 100 instead of a letter grade, although your report will show letter grades and a GPA.

The conversion is usually:

Letter	Number	GPA	Letter	Number	GPA
A+ =	97-100	(4.0)	B+ =	87-89	(3.3)
A =	93-96	(4.0)	B =	83-86	(3.0)
A- =	90-92	(3.7)	B- =	80-82	(2.7)
C+ =	77-79	(2.3)	D+ =	67-69	(1.3)
C =	73-76	(2.0)	D =	65-66	(1.0)
C- =	70-72	(1.7)	F =	below 65	(Fail)

Grades can also include an I (Incomplete) and a W (Withdrawal).

To calculate your GPA :

★ Convert your marks out of 100 or letter grades into the corresponding GPA number e.g. A+ = 4.0.

★ Multiply this number by the number of credit/ hours for the class, e.g. a class of three credit hours in which you received an A+ would be 3 x 4.0 = 12.

★ For your overall GPA, add up all classes and grades this way and divide the total by the total number of credit/ hours you are taking.

For example, if you are taking three classes for three credit hours each, and you receive an A, B, and C respectively, your calculation would be:

A grade = 4.0 Multiply by 3 (credit hours)   = 12.0
B grade = 3.3 Multiply by 3   = 9.9
C grade = 2.0 Multiply by 3   = 6.0
                                    Total = 27.9

Divide the total (27.9) by the number of credit hours (9) to get the overall GPA = 3.1

Most colleges stipulate a minimum GPA required to graduate, although some colleges do not calculate a GPA at all.

 TIP
Some colleges assign different weight to more difficult classes so check with your own college for details on variations when calculating your GPA.

Grading on a curve

Grading on a curve (*curving*) refers to the statistical method of 'bell curve grading', whereby students are graded according to their performance when compared to others in the class. Curved grading takes the highest score in a test or class and ranks everyone by that maximum. In such cases, the top 10% of scores receive an A, the next 20% a B, and the remaining 70% receive a C or lower. If you scored 87% in a test (which would be a B without the curve) but the highest score was 90%, you'd most likely receive an A grade when curved.

Pass/ fail

In some instances you can take a class and receive only a pass or a fail. The class will still count toward your credit hour total but your GPA will not be affected. Students take such classes if they are worried about the grade they will receive but need the credit, or if they want to take a class but don't need the added stress of worrying about the grade. It is not recommended that you take too many of these, as the pass/ fail result shows up on your final transcript.

Examinations

Although most college students are graded on year-round work (essays and participation), there are also end-of-year exams and midterms. Most professors also give additional smaller tests throughout the year. Shorter tests are often referred to as *quizzes*, but don't be fooled into thinking they are fun little tests – they can also count toward your GPA. You may hear reference to a *pop quiz*, which has nothing to do with music, and means a test in class with no prior warning:

★ **Exams**. Exams can either be *open book* or *closed book*, meaning you are allowed to take your textbooks or notes in, or you're not allowed anything.

★ **Online tests**. Some professors allow you to take a test on your computer in your own time, outside of the classroom (i.e. in your dorm room or the library). Obviously you are not allowed to have anyone else take the test for you, or otherwise enlist help from your peers unless specifically permitted.

★ **Midterms**. These exams occur about halfway through the academic term or semester and are as important as the end of year finals. They are not to be confused with *mock* exams.

★ **Reading period**. Many education establishments have a reading week or a reading period prior to exams, when there are no classes, no new material is taught and the time is set aside for exam preparation. Students often refer to this period as *Dead week* or *Hell week* and colleges often halt extra-curricular activities and emphasize quiet at this time. It is not advised to leave all exam studying till the reading period as many professors also assign term papers at the same time.

Your professor (or TA) will tell you what portion of the syllabus will be included in upcoming tests and exams – ask for this information if it's not forthcoming. Don't assume end-of-year finals will cover the entire academic year's syllabus, as many only cover the second semester's work. You will usually be advised what percentage of your grade exams, papers, labs and presentations account for.

Office hours

Office hours are the times when a professor is specifically available to his or her students. These hours are usually listed with class information and they can be drop-in or by appointment only. Even if they are drop-in, it is advisable and courteous to send your professor an e-mail to make sure s/ he will be there. If you can't make the posted office hours, you can still contact the professor to make an appointment for another time. When meeting a professor during office hours, be sensitive to the needs of any other students waiting to see him or her. Keep chitchat to a minimum and get to the point quickly.

Tutoring

If you are struggling in any subject, there is help at hand. Most colleges have a free tutoring program or Learning Center where you can receive help, usually from another college student. A quick search on your college web site ('Tutoring') will bring up everything you need to know. At some colleges the assistance is one-on-one and you'll need to fill out a formal request and register with the tutoring program. At other colleges it might be a drop-in situation where you don't need an appointment. I advise you find out when the busiest times are likely to be, as this might mean you won't get as much individual assistance as you need.

Graduation

Graduation is commonly known as *Commencement* at colleges in the USA, although it occurs at the end of an academic year. Commencement is the conferring of degrees on graduating students, and the information on the web site is usually under the 'Commencement' tab. There is no need to go into detail about Commencement here, as you will have four years to learn more on your own:

★ At most colleges Commencement is a big deal and spans several days. At very large colleges the actual degree ceremony will be held at the individual schools, with perhaps a larger school ceremony before or after. There will also be activities for visiting family members.

★ Commencement ceremony speakers are huge in the US, with many colleges paying big bucks for big names. Examples include Meryl Streep, who spoke at Barnard College in 2010, Bono at the University of Pennsylvania in 2004, JK Rowling at Harvard University in 2008, and Tom Hanks at Yale University in 2011.

Study abroad

In American colleges the Study Abroad program refers to students studying in a foreign country for a term/ semester or a whole year. This experience is usually counted as part of their American degree and they receive college credit hours for it. Naturally, Study Abroad programs and requirements differ from one college to the next, but most college web sites have a specific page devoted to this information, which should be your starting point if you are interested in this opportunity.

American students usually wait until their sophomore or junior year (years 2 and 3) to study abroad. Many colleges have seminars about the Study Abroad programs on offer, with students present who have already taken advantage of the program who are available to advise you. It's a good idea to attend a seminar and/ or talk to students who've already done this. You'll find there are several things to take into consideration when looking at the options:

★ **Fees**. Although your college tuition fees may not increase, there is often a *program fee*. You may also be expected to pay for housing, meals etc. while abroad. In some cases there will be a significant increase in your college tuition fee for the time you are abroad. Remember to factor in your airfare to and from the new country.

★ **Visa standing**. If the foreign country in question requires a visa your International Students Office (ISO) may not be able to help. The visa required will relate to your nationality and will not be under the jurisdiction of the US government. In most cases though, the ISO will be able to point you in the right direction – if not, your first port of call should be your country's embassy in Washington DC.

★ **Existing scholarships**. If you are in receipt of any type of scholarship, you should check with the funding body to see if this will be affected by your temporary absence. If the scholarship has come from your college, check with the Financial Aid office or the department granting it.

★ **Potential scholarships**. Many college web sites report a number of scholarships available to students wanting to study abroad. Check with the Study Abroad office or staff member to see if you are eligible.

★ **Country options**. Many colleges have reciprocal arrangements set up with colleges from other countries, and you are limited to these options. Other colleges allow you to do your own research and make suggestions about where you might study. Make sure to find out what the situation is before you start planning too far ahead.

★ **Academic choices** while abroad. Discuss your potential choice of classes with your academic advisor to make sure they are complementary to your studies at your American college, and you will be given credit for them. You will probably be required to take the same amount of credit hours that you would if you were still in the USA, and to stay on track for graduation, these classes should help fulfill your gradation requirements.

★ **Transfer of credits**. Your study abroad semester, term or year should still allow you to accrue the credits you need to graduate. When planning your program make sure it will give you college credits, otherwise it may affect the timing of your graduation. If you won't gain as many credits as you would by staying in the USA, remember many colleges have summer classes for their undergraduate students, and this may be a way for you to catch up.

★ **Transfer of records**. If on a program that is well established and reciprocal with your college, academic record keeping shouldn't be an issue. However, if you are putting a program together yourself, it is important to ensure the academic records of your time spent studying abroad can be transferred back to your American college. You should also make sure you can access a record of your time at a foreign academic institution when you are applying for graduate degree programs or positions of employment in the future. In most cases your American college will not be the institution providing these records.

General information

Spring break

This is a big deal at many colleges and is traditionally the time when students converge on unsuspecting beach towns in Florida and beyond. Fortunately spring break isn't the same countrywide – your week off will depend on your college's academic calendar.

If you plan to leave the USA during spring break, don't forget to obtain a Travel Signature before your departure and find out if you'll need a visa to enter your destination country. (See beginning of this chapter for details.)

Health and well-being

Your college most likely has a student health center or provides medical services of some type. Although you might be charged per visit, if you think you have a communicable health issue such as a throat infection (commonly called *strep throat*), or the more serious mononucleosis (*glandular fever* to some), you should schedule an appointment as soon as possible and get yourself treated. Yes, you're very busy, but putting off a health visit often results in more lost time as your condition worsens. Besides, the only way to prevent illness spreading through campus is to seek treatment as soon as possible:

★ Your college (or the health center) will also provide *mental health* services. Other terms that might be used at your college include *counseling* and *therapy*. If you have any type of emotional problem (e.g. stress, depression) and feel unable to cope, do not hesitate to call on this confidential support system. A phone number will be available on the college web site and probably posted around campus. There will also be someone *on call* so you can receive support at any time of the day or night.

★ In American culture there is no shame or embarrassment in receiving mental health support and because these services are confidential, no one need find out if you wish to keep it quiet. The most important thing is that you talk to someone about your concerns or your situation. Amanda Ecklar, of Yale University's Office for International Students and Scholars, finds that reluctance to use the mental health services on campus occasionally leads international students to drop out. "Every year someone goes home because of a breakdown and nobody else knew about it." No one will know if you seek counseling except the counselor – do not let your fear of being shamed or embarrassed prevent you from getting help.

★ If you have to pay at the time of the visit, keep all paperwork, as you will probably be able to submit it to your health insurance company and be reimbursed for some or all of the cost. Health insurance policies often run on the calendar year so you should submit your paperwork before the December 31 deadline.

Parental input

As I tell your parents in *Chapter Twelve – Notes for Parents*, many American colleges encourage a lot more parental involvement than your peers back home probably have to tolerate. Fortunately for you, given the distance from your home country, your parents will likely not be as involved as some of the American parents you will meet.

Don't be surprised to find your college sends regular e-mails to your parents about everything from campus security to the bands playing each week. You'll be pleased to know it's not typical (and often not legal), for colleges to e-mail parents about your personal activities and academic performance without your permission.

Sports

The college sports scene in the USA is huge. Almost every college has *varsity* teams for many sports and loyal, passionate fans. Some campuses revolve around their college sports, while others have a less intense focus, but almost every college web site has a page devoted to its sports, and the big sports are televised.

There are also intramural sports which are not played at the college level, but students compete against other individuals or teams within the college.

Transportation

Most college campuses have their own transportation for students. Not only do these services ferry students from one end of campus to the other, they often provide free rides to the nearest towns and shopping malls. The information will be available at the college web site and usually at one of the campus offices.

Chapter Eleven
The American Language and Customs

Whether or not English is your first language, if you didn't grow up in the USA you have a few things to learn about the American way of life. This chapter covers the basics to help you negotiate your first few weeks of college life, but you'll probably find your whole four years at college will be full of discoveries and surprises.

Culture shock

No matter how thrilled you are to be studying in the USA you will probably experience culture shock at some point, and this is perfectly normal. There are many aspects of life in the US, which are completely different from anywhere else – from the pace of life to how to make friends, there is a lot to get used to. Juliana Tamayo, a Columbian undergraduate remembers, "I think the first semester was the hardest, mostly because college level classes were hard to get used to. Living in dorms and having a random roommate was also very difficult. At first I thought I would never get used to such a different culture, but by spring semester it was all much better."

Indian student Tanya Rehki remembers, "When I first arrived I was in extreme culture shock, it was nothing like I imagined it to be. Nothing was remotely similar to the environment I grew up in."

Experts on culture shock have written hundreds of books about the subject, and your International Students Office should have material and support services for you:

★ You might think that acknowledging culture shock is a sign of weakness, but denial can lead to real problems. While you should allow yourself to feel homesick and perhaps even scared, if you're feeling extremely isolated, confused or depressed try to take steps to deal with the situation before it gets worse.

★ Don't forget almost everyone at your college is going through a major life change. Even for American students, this is a new phase of their lives – many are far from home, have arrived at a college where they know few or no other people and could possibly be experiencing cultural differences too. British student Joe Holleran admits his biggest concern was arriving at a college where he knew no one. Although this concern vanished on arrival, "As everyone was helpful and welcoming," he also used his graduating class' Facebook page to introduce himself and get his questions answered. Joe remembers it took about two months before he felt settled in the USA. He adds, "I felt as if the whole soccer thing helped me out quite a bit and being from a different country really helps you stand out in your classes… to gain friends and support from your professors."

★ Make the effort to attend every seminar or gathering intended for the groups to which you belong – international students, members of your department and residents in your dorm. All will help you meet new people and understand the environment you now find yourself in.

★ Try to find a balance between mixing with students from your home country and mixing with American students. International students often stick together especially when they first arrive on campus – although this may prevent a sense of isolation, it can delay your settling in and feeling less of a stranger in the USA. Tanya Rehki says, "For the first year at my college I was constantly uneasy and unsure about how to conduct myself, but the more friends I made the easier my life became. I realized a support system is extremely important in order to feel in place. In the first year most freshman are friendless and it's hard to go about each day."

★ The teaching style in US colleges may add to any culture shock you may experience. Tanya Rehki adds, "The learning style in the US is very lecture oriented and professors do not involve themselves with the students. In my high-school teachers and students were as close as students were to each other. The learning environment was more interactive and aided our learning process. I felt more support from teachers in my high school than I do here… Moving countries is not something you can study for and the challenges will be unexpected. But if you come in with an open mind you are more likely to combine with the culture, instead of going against the grain."

Many Americans have never traveled outside the USA and may not know much about your home country. This doesn't mean they aren't interested in your country and your culture, so try not to see this as ignorant or insulting. The USA is a huge country and Americans love traveling around it, enjoying the vastly different regions, cultures and climates. Americans also have relatively small vacation allowances, which often preclude traveling too far from home, and flights from the USA to far-flung countries are expensive.

No matter what your initial thoughts are about the American way of doing things, looking down on all things American, or otherwise implying things aren't done properly in the US, tends to cause offence. Americans are very patriotic and will argue vehemently in favor of the USA when presented with dissenting opinions. Although it's natural, when going through culture shock, to pick fault with things in your host country, try not to voice every negative thought. Better still, try to look upon these strange things as interesting and different rather than weird or wrong.

📖 FURTHER READING
You can read more about culture shock at these web sites:

The Consortium for International Education and MultiCultural Studies – http://www.worldwide.edu/travel_planner/culture_shock.html.

At this site international students talk about their first experiences on coming to the USA to study – http://internationallife.wikispaces.com/culture+shock+stories

---

Homesickness

Homesickness is inevitable for most new undergraduates, even if they're from the USA. Students Joe and Juliana (see above) had different ways of dealing with it.

Joe recalls, "I noticed everyone kept in touch with me in the first semester, which made me miss home. But once the novelty wore off, many friends didn't contact me everyday – which helps a lot, believe it or not! It's important to pull through the first few months – and make sure parents visits are held off until at least one month after you head off to college in freshman year (my plan) – I wanted to be left on my own to be forced to adapt and meet people, rather than missing such opportunities."

Juliana had a slightly different approach, "Try to keep an open mind and be sure to keep in contact with your parents and friends back home – don't be afraid to say you miss home, it's okay to do so and I think everyone does anyway."

Repatriation

American citizens who have lived abroad and return to the USA for college often go through a specific type of culture shock called repatriation. Unlike other international students, they may arrive on campus expecting to fit in because they lived in the US as a child, have an American accent, have attended American schools abroad or perhaps one or both parents is American and they have visited family in the US frequently. The experience of many repatriating students is their global background sets them apart from other American students. If you are in this category, don't be surprised to find yourself not quite fitting in, and again, be prepared to acknowledge your feelings and seek help if you feel yourself getting too overwhelmed by them.

Kareem Osman is an American student who lived briefly in the USA before relocating to various countries around the world. Although he comes to the USA every year and experienced no great culture shock, there were other surprises. "It was an easier process for me, having been to American schools and coming to the States a lot, but it was the first time being in the USA, surrounded mainly by Americans and their attitude to foreigners surprised me. I grew up hearing a lot of different accents so it seemed weird that the American students, for example, constantly commented on my Australian friend's accent."

📖 **FURTHER READING**
The Global Nomad's Guide to University Transition by Tina L. Quick (Summertime Publishing) is a comprehensive

resource written for teens who have lived overseas and who are returning to their 'home' country for college. The sound advice given by Quick is also applicable to foreign students attending an overseas university.

Greetings

One of the first thing's you'll notice is that many Americans make eye contact and greet people as they pass them in the street, dorm hallway or classroom – even people they have never met before. It is considered rude to avoid eye contact by looking down or looking away, and if you don't feel comfortable in replying you should at least smile to acknowledge their words:

★ The words you'll hear can be anything from 'Hi' to 'How's it going?' and 'How are you?' While you do need to acknowledge the greeting, it's not necessary to stop and give a full run down of your day or week. For the most part other Americans will reply, 'Great, how are *you*?' and keep going about their business. It's not so much a question as a greeting in itself.

★ Younger Americans can often be heard addressing their elders as 'Sir' and 'Ma'am' (to rhyme with *ham*), which may seem strange to non-Americans. While it isn't required by anyone, it is a very convenient way to catch someone's attention when you don't know his or her name. If someone has dropped something in the street, the quickest way to let someone know is to say 'Sir' or 'Ma'am' while helping to retrieve the item.

⚠ WARNING

Addressing someone below the age of about 40 as 'Sir' or 'Ma'am' is probably not advisable and certainly won't make that person feel great.

★ Although not many Americans greet each other with kisses, there is a lot of hugging. Girls will hug each other when they meet and when they say goodbye – don't be surprised if a female student you have just met hugs you when it's time to leave. In general, guys shake hands on meeting, but with good friends are also known to give each other giant bear hugs. Between young male students, particularly fraternity brothers, you may see ritualistic fist bump greetings, involving elaborate hand movements.

★ Relationships with college professors, while respectful, will probably seem fairly informal to some international students. American students are encouraged to ask questions and in some cases to challenge what professors are saying, so students will not seem as deferential as you may be used to. In general, students do not hug their professors on meeting them and they address them as Professor or Doctor unless specifically told to use first names. They may be on first name terms with teaching assistants, but generally not with professors, although they may address both as 'Sir' or 'Ma'am'.

★ On the phone, although you'll quickly learn that Americans move at a fairly rapid pace, when phoning someone they don't typically dive straight into the conversation. Instead they will ask how the other person is and generally chitchat for a few minutes. Only then will the caller get round to the real reason for the call. In emergencies, when there is no time for small talk, the caller will apologize for seeming rude, before launching into the subject.

Language, vocabulary and spelling tips

There's a well known saying by the late Irish dramatist, George Bernard Shaw: '*England and America are two countries separated by a common language*', and if you grew up speaking British English you'll quickly find it's true. Even if you grew up learning American English as your

223

second language, there are a lot of idioms and abbreviations that may not have been part of your studies. (There are also words and phrases specific to college life, which have been covered in previous chapters.)

Euphemisms

Americans use euphemisms that often mask what's really going on. When I first came to the USA I frequently came out of meetings not really knowing what had been decided. I was used to a more frank exchange, and the careful phrasing of my American colleagues often left me clueless.

Some of the more common euphemisms are:

★ *Blowing smoke* – tricking someone or covering something up.
★ *Bought the farm* – when someone is said to have bought the farm, or bought it, they have died. The origins of this phrase are not certain but Google it for a few suggestions.
★ *Disposable Mucus Recovery Systems* (seriously) – Kleenex/ tissues. I'm including this as an extreme example, in case you ever come across it.
★ *Has issues* – is as mad as a hatter. Perhaps it's not quite that bad, but when you hear someone 'has issues', it's usually not complimentary. The alternative to this phrase is 'has a lot of baggage'. This usually means they have had a harrowing life or a lot of failed relationships – in either case it prevents them from being normal.
★ *I hear what you're saying, but…* – usually means the speaker doesn't agree with a word you've said and is about to give you his or her opinion.
★ *Low self-esteem* – depressed, unhappy. Americans use this phrase a lot, either as a put down or to explain someone who is making very bad decisions, such as drug abuse.
★ *Passed away* – people never 'die' and the few times I've used this word, it almost caused a physical, shocked reaction. Even when

a person dies a very sudden death, it's still referred to as 'passed away'. The only exception to this seems to be when a famous person dies and it's announced on TV. Then it's, "John Doe, dead at the age of 92."

★ *Self-medicates* – drinks too much or uses drugs. The meaning behind this phrase is that someone is trying to deal with his or her problems with drugs or alcohol.

★ *Wardrobe malfunction* – a slip of the clothes revealing too much of one's body. A tongue-in-cheek reference to Janet Jackson's breast revealing episode at the Superbowl a few years ago. If someone tells you you're having a wardrobe malfunction, check all zippers and buttons.

Spelling

There are many spelling differences between British and American English, so use the American spell-checker on your computer, and purchase a good American dictionary when you arrive in the USA. It might help to find out how much weight is given to spelling in the papers you submit, if you speak or have learned British English:

★ *Ou*. In general, where there is a word with *ou* in British English, the American version drops the *u* – so *colour* becomes *color*, *honour* becomes *honor*, *neighbour* becomes *neighbor* and so on.

★ *Re*. Words that you might end with *re*, are typically reversed in the USA. *Theatre* becomes *theater* (except when people are trying to be artsy), *centre* becomes *center* and *sombre* becomes *somber*.

★ *Ogue*. Words ending in *ogue* in British English usually drop the *ue* in American English in everyday usage. *Catalogue* frequently becomes *catalog*, and *monologue*, *monolog* – although Webster's dictionary cites either version as acceptable.

★ *Double LL*. Words that obtain an extra *l* when elongated, usually stick with a single *l* in American English. Although both spell *travel* with one *l*, in American English extensions don't double up, so it's *traveler* and *traveled*. Likewise, although it's wool on both sides of the Atlantic, the American extension is woolen. In addition, many words with a double *ll* in British English only have one l in American English. Examples include *counselor* and *marvelous*. To confuse the matter further, there are some words which contain a double *ll* in American English where it's a single *l* in British English, so what you might know as *enrol* becomes *enroll*.

★ **Neighboring vowels.** Many words with consecutive vowels in British English only contain one of those vowels in American English. Thus, there is no *a* as the second letter of *pediatric*, and *diarrhea* is slightly easier to spell.

★ **S becomes Z.** Probably one of the best-known differences between British and American English is the switch from *s* to *z* at the end of many words. Examples include *appetizer*, *criticize*, *authorize*, and *analyze*.

 TIP
For British English speakers – the letter Z is pronounced *zee* rather than *zed*. If you say *zed*, chances are no one will understand you.

In American English a sentence ends with a *period*, not a full-stop, and it may or may not contain *quotation marks* instead of inverted commas, and *parentheses* rather than brackets.

Pronunciation

Again, if you speak British English, you'll find many common words are pronounced differently in the USA. For the most part this makes for interesting conversation, but from time to time it can cause confusion.

> ⚠️ **WARNING**
> British English speakers should remember the adage, 'Not wrong, just different'. When you come across an unfamiliar pronunciation don't automatically assume your version is the right one. Some American English words and phrases come from very old English and it's actually British English that has moved farther away from its root.

Because of the proliferation of American TV shows and blockbuster movies, people from around the world are used to hearing American accents. Not so the other way round. Even the most cut glass English accent sounds unfamiliar to many Americans and Australian, Kiwi or South African accents are similarly confusing. If you don't speak like an American you are advised to slow down when talking in the USA, particularly when you're on the phone. That's not to say your accent is a negative. There are many immigrants in the USA, all speaking English with different accents. Your foreign accent is no big deal, so don't be shy about voicing your opinion and otherwise speaking up.

A few differences between British and American English pronunciations are:

★ **The long A.** Generally this doesn't exist in the States. British English words like *staff*, *laugh*, *bath* and *grass* may not be understood if pronounced with the long A. An exception that comes to mind is *pasta*, which Americans give a long A (rhyming with the British English *master*) rather than a flat A.

★ **Vowel sounds.** Sometimes American English is very different from British English in terms of vowel pronunciation. Examples include:
  - Names like Sonia – the *o* is pronounced more like the sound in toe.
  - Van Gogh – is pronounced *Van Go*.
  - *Basil* becomes *bay-zil*, *herb* has no audible *h*, *yogurt* loses the h

227

and is pronounced *yow-gurt*, and *risotto* is pronounced *ris-ow-tow* (both as in *row* your boat).

- Tomato as you probably know, is pronounced tom-ay-tow, and more often tom-ay-do. If you pronounce it the British way it's sometimes easier just to point when you're ordering a sandwich.

★ **Consonants**. Consonants can also cause confusion when you're not used to hearing the American version. As you probably know, a *t* often has more of a *d* sound, making it difficult to know if someone's name is *Matty* or *Maddy*. Alternatively, sometimes the t has no sound at all, which means *winter* can often sound like *winner*. To complicate matters further, regional accents vary greatly within the USA. Always best to pay attention so you can understand the context of the words you're hearing.

📖 **FURTHER READING**
If you're really into words and everything about them, visit Michael Quinion's excellent web site World Wide Words – http://www.worldwidewords.org/

Vocabulary

There will probably be many American words that are new to you, and it's impossible to include them all in this book. As I have advised earlier, buy yourself a good American dictionary or find a good web site so you're never stumped by a strange word.

📖 **FURTHER READING**
Merriam Webster is a reliable American dictionary and thesaurus with a web site and free apps – www.meriam-webster.com

One expression you'll hear in the USA that might not be familiar to you is Holidays, not to be confused with vacations. You will hear other students asking, "What are you doing for the holidays?" Holidays refers to Thanksgiving, which is always the fourth Thursday in November and it is a huge occasion in the USA. College classes will usually finish at noon on the Wednesday, and you won't be expected back till the following Monday. Many students will go home, as Thanksgiving is a big family get-together. Holidays also refers to the Christmas and Hanukah period in December, another time when students go back to their family homes for the winter vacation.

General information

Although explaining all the differences you'll find in the USA is another book entirely, the following information will be useful to you in the first weeks and months.

Dates

Americans write the month first when writing the date in numbers. This is very important to know when filling in paperwork, writing checks and understanding deadlines.

Therefore 4/10/2013 is April 10, 2013. Most Americans will not know the reverse version exists, so if you make a mistake they will not catch it as an international error.

Dining

In your first few weeks of college you will most likely be eating in campus cafeterias:

★ These are self-serve restaurants where you take a tray and choose your food from a wide range on offer. Some of the food may be unfamiliar to you – take your time and don't be afraid to ask questions. This may be a great time to befriend an American student who can tell you what everything is.

★ When you have a tray full of food, take it to the checkout where you will either be asked to swipe your dining card or pay in cash.

★ When you have finished your meal, look around to see if there are large trash receptacles with trays on top. This usually means you should clear up your own plate, utensils, and tray, and is often to referred to as *bussing your table*.

If you go to a restaurant to eat there may be some things that are unfamiliar to you:

★ Depending how busy your local town or city is, you may have to make a reservation at a restaurant. Most restaurants have web sites where you can find the phone number or reserve your table online. If family members are planning to visit when lots of other student families are also in town, it's advisable to book ahead for dinner.

★ Some restaurants do not take reservations, or only allow you to reserve a table if you have a party of perhaps six or more people. If it's a popular restaurant you may want to allow yourselves at least 30 minutes wait time. Ask around to find out how busy the restaurants are.

★ Unless the restaurant specifically states '*Please take a seat*' it's common to wait until a waiter or the Maitre D approaches you and shows you to a table. Even with casual looking places make sure a staff member has seen you before you take a seat, so s/ he will know to come and take your order.

★ In some restaurants the person who comes and puts bread on your table, fills your glass with water and so on, is called a *busboy* and isn't always the person who will be taking your order. If this person doesn't attempt to take your order it means your waiter or waitress is coming. Similarly, if you need something throughout the meal you must catch the attention of the waiter who initially took your order, rather than the *busboy* or a waiter from another table. In medium to large restaurants the wait staff are usually in charge of small sections of a restaurant, and do not attend to everyone.

★ Typically you'll be given a menu and asked what you would like to drink. The waiter will give you a few minutes to look over the menu, bring your drinks and then ask what you'd like to order.

> ⚠ **WARNING**
> If you order alcohol and don't appear to be 21 or older, you will be asked to provide photo ID. If you attempt to buy alcohol for another member of your party, this person will also be carded. Many establishments card people who could be older than the minimum age, just to be on the safe side.

★ All but the most expensive restaurants in the USA expect you to eat your meal and leave promptly. Although you are not given a time slot, such as 7-9 pm, if you linger at the table after you have finished your meal, you will be presented with the bill. Although you will hear, "I'll take that whenever you're ready" if you still linger the waiter will repeatedly ask if he or she can get you anything else, which is a big hint you should vacate the table.

★ American portions are generally large and you will often find you can't finish a meal. It is both common (and acceptable), to ask for this food to be *wrapped* or *boxed*, to take with you to eat later. When ordering you can also ask to split a dish with a friend, if you think the portion would feed more than one person. If in doubt waiters are usually very honest when telling you how big or small a portion is.

★ The price you see at the very bottom of the bill is the price you are required to pay – taxes will already be included in the total. In some instances a gratuity (tip) or service charge has already been added, but usually there will be an empty line above the total where you are expected to add your tip if paying with a card. If you are paying in cash, leave your payment and tip with the bill. If you only have large notes your waiter may ask you if you need change – if the amount of the large notes is more than you want to leave as a tip, answer yes, and then take your tip from the change you receive. This is very common and not at all embarrassing.

★ In more casual restaurants and diners you may have to take your bill up to the front desk to pay. If so, either leave a tip before you leave the table, or go back after paying and leave it then. In most restaurants it is safe to leave the tip on the table.

★ A tip is between 15 and 20% of the bill. Many waiters and waitresses work for less than minimum wage and it is assumed they will make up the amount with tips. You will notice very few Americans leave no tip at all, no matter how bad the food or the service, although they do not hesitate to send food back if they feel it is not cooked properly or not what they asked for.

★ You will find you eat at sandwich bars quite often on campus. These sandwiches are usually made while you wait and to your specifications. It is advisable to study the menu first before attempting to order, because you will be hit with rapid-fire questions as to what type of bread, fillings and dressings you'd like. If you haven't a clue, this will irritate everyone around you and probably cause you to order something you don't really want.

Americans do not tip at food counters, coffee bars and sandwich bars.

Drinking

You must be 21 years of age to purchase or drink alcohol in every state in the USA, and you may not buy alcohol for anyone else under the minimum age:

★ If you attempt to get into bars most will ask for photo ID, called *carding*. Many bars won't admit underage people, but some will let you in and stamp the back of your hand so you can't buy alcohol.

★ Many bars have waiters and waitresses who come around to the tables, although you can also approach the bar and order drinks there.

★ It is customary to leave a small tip after buying a round of drinks. You can leave the tip on the bar or give it to your waiter when paying. Don't leave anything less than one dollar.

 WARNING
Remember, as an international student getting into trouble for underage drinking could put you out of visa status and lead to deportation at your expense.

Menus

When you pick up a menu almost anywhere, there will probably be items you're not familiar with. Although the USA is one country, because of its vast size, there are often menu items only seen in certain parts of the country. Grits, for example, can be found on many southern menus, but unless it's a themed restaurant, they're not too common farther north, east and west. If you're ever in doubt about a menu item, ask the waiter what it is and you'll get a detailed description right down to how it's cooked and served:

★ The first, small course is the appetizer, although some are big enough to serve as a full meal. It is perfectly acceptable to order only an appetizer, or to ask for two appetizers as your meal. You can often order appetizers 'for the table', where all the plates are put in the middle and everyone shares.

★ The main course is called the entrée (pronounced 'ontray'), and they are often enormous. You don't usually have to order an entrée if you feel there will be too much food, although don't forget you can ask for food to be *wrapped* or *boxed* if you want to take it home to eat later.

★ The sweet course is called dessert and again, the portions can be quite large. It is very common to order one or two desserts to share, and the waiter will bring as many spoons, forks and small plates as there are people at the table.

★ Describing individual menu items in the USA is beyond the scope of this book, but I promise there is nothing on the menu that is too gross. Although some Americans eat pigs' feet, most menu items are fairly harmless and you can usually tell what you're eating. The biggest surprise for foreigners is that generally Americans have a very sweet tooth so many foods are sweeter than they're used to.

Money

The American currency is dollars and cents, the symbol for each being $ and ¢:

★ Paper money (notes) comes in $1, $5, $10, $20, $50 and $100 bills. All are the same size and almost the same color, making it difficult for foreigners to tell them apart at first. Each note has a different historical figure on one side, which often becomes the nickname

for that note:
- A dollar bill features George Washington, the first President of the USA
- A $5 bill has Abraham Lincoln, the sixteenth President of the USA
- A $10 bill features Alexander Hamilton, the first American Secretary of State
- The $20 bill shows President Andrew Jackson, the seventh President of the USA
- The $50 bill features President Ulysses S Grant, the eighteenth President of the USA
- The $100 has Benjamin Franklin, one of the Founding Fathers of the USA
- There is also a $2 bill but it is not common

★ Coins are not all the same size and can either be silver or copper colored:
- The smallest coin is the dime or 10¢, which is silver colored
- The next size up is the one-cent piece, which is copper colored and sometimes referred to as a penny
- Next is the nickel or 5¢ coin, which is silver colored
- The largest coin is the quarter or 25¢ coin, which is silver colored
- There are also dollar and half dollar (fifty cent) coins but they are not common

★ There are many nicknames for American money: the most common are *buck*, *clam* and *greenback* for a dollar; one thousand dollars is often called a *grand*; money in general is commonly referred to as *dough* and *moolah*.

★ Obviously the exchange rate against other world currencies varies.

Public transport

If you come from a country with good public transportation you might be in for a shock in the USA, particularly if you attend a college in a small town or in the middle of nowhere. Public *transit* (as it's often known) can be very patchy in the USA. To find information for your city, town or area online, type in the location and 'transit'. Most web sites will give you details of all the services, routes, timetables, and trip planners informing passengers how to get from one location to another:

★ **Bus services**. Many big cities have a bus service that is usually inexpensive and easy to use. You can buy travel cards instead of having to buy a ticket every time you board a bus, and there are often student discounts. Look on the web site under 'Fares' to find out about discounts – you may have to purchase a card from your college rather than the transit authority.

★ **Light rail**. Some larger cities have underground or over ground rail services, often referred to as *light rail*. These are under the auspices of the local transit authority. You can often use the same travel pass for bus and train services within one city.

★ **Cabs and taxis**. Cab or taxi service in the USA depends heavily on your location. In some large cities, like Chicago, New York and Washington DC, you can hail a cab in the street. In other locations you may have to call or go online to book a cab. Always ask when the estimated time of arrival is and what the approximate fare will be to your destination:

- When catching a cab on the street, get into the back of the cab from the sidewalk side of the car and tell the driver your destination. Sometimes the driver will ask which route you want to take – this means there are a number of ways to drive to your destination and s/ he is asking if you have a preference. If you have a preference then state it, and if you don't, ask the driver what difference one route will make over the other. Sometimes drivers ask this in case you want to avoid heavy traffic or take the scenic route.
- When you arrive at your destination, pay the driver from the back of the cab. The fare should be displayed on the meter in the front of the cab. It is customary to tip taxi drivers about 15% of the fare.

- If you have luggage the driver will either get out of the cab to put it in the trunk (boot), or will pop the trunk open so you can do this. When you have paid for your cab ride the driver will retrieve the luggage from the trunk.
- Always look back to make sure you haven't left anything on the seat of the taxi. It is a good idea to make a note of the taxi number as you get in, but as many people don't, it's safer not to leave anything behind.

★ **Amtrak**. The national rail service is called Amtrak and can take you from one end of the country to the other – http://www.amtrak.com. Most of the trains are not high speed, so the journeys can be very long and are not particularly cheap. It can be less expensive to fly.

★ **Long distance buses**. The most well known inter-city bus service is Greyhound Lines – www.greyhound.com. You can purchase tickets at the many Greyhound terminals around the country. Another national bus company is Megabus, which is popular with students as it often has service to smaller college towns – http://us.megabus.com/.

★ **Flying within the US**. Flying from one city to another is very common in the USA although not as inexpensive or convenient as it used to be. The airline you fly with will often depend on where you are located, as many do not fly out of every airport. It pays to search for flight and fare options on web sites such as Expedia, Kayak, Fare Compare and so on, but you should always check back with the suggested airline's own site – they often match the fares and may be able to offer more scheduling options.

Shopping

No matter where you're from, the American shopping experience is probably different from your native country. Here are a few pointers to help you navigate the process:

★ **Customer service**. The USA is known for great customer service, but it can sometimes feel overwhelming if you're not used to extremely attentive sales assistants. Often there is a greeter standing near the doorway who will welcome you as you enter. If they ask you how you are, it's just a way of greeting you, so a big smile or a "Fine thanks" is all that's needed as a response. Sometimes they will ask you if you're looking for something in particular – if you are, tell them and you'll be taken to the correct section of the store. If you want to wander around or don't want the attention, tell the sales person you're browsing and they will usually back off.

★ **Checking bags**. Some stores will ask you to *check* any bags you may be carrying before you are allowed to shop or browse. This is a theft prevention measure. Take your bag to wherever they indicate – you will hand your bag over and be given a numbered ticket. Before you exit the store, take this ticket back to the same place to retrieve your bag. You are usually only asked to check shopping bags from other stores, and you should never hand over a bag containing money, credit cards, valuables or other personal items.

★ **Giving out e-mail and phone numbers**. Many stores will ask for an e-mail address when they take payment – this is to add you to the marketing list and is not required to complete the sale. If you don't want to give them your e-mail address for any reason, just say "No thank you". Sometimes the store will send you coupons via e-mail but they also sell your address to marketing companies, which could mean a lot of spam in the future. Similarly, you will often be asked for a phone number, which you don't have to give unless you are paying by check.

★ **Personal checks**. Many stores will not accept personal checks and those that do will require photo ID and probably an accompanying credit card.

★ **Credit card payments**. While sales assistants usually don't do a particularly thorough job of matching signatures on credit cards, you may be asked for a second form of ID. This is often a driving license with photo, so remember to carry yours – if you don't have a driving license and they don't accept your college ID, you should use your passport.

★ **Bargaining/ haggling**. This is generally not the norm in American stores, although if you buy an item that is slightly flawed you can ask for a discounted price. In most instances where you receive a discount you will be told the sale is 'final'. This means you cannot return the item for any reason.

★ **Returns**. It is normally easy to return merchandise in the USA. Remember to keep your receipt and return the item within the specified time (usually a month or 30 days). Sometimes stores will offer you a store credit instead of money back, which means you must buy something else from the store, either at the time of the return or some time in the future. You may find you have more trouble returning something that is broken (as opposed to not wanted), but stand your ground and explain your problem. The store might try to offer you a replacement, but if you are not interested in the same product tell them you would like your money back. If you are planning to buy an expensive item, find out what the store's return policy is before you buy it.

★ **Extended warranties**. When buying electric appliances, computers and so on, sales assistants will often offer an *extended warranty* with it. Many of these items are already guaranteed for one year after the purchase date, but the extended warranty offers protection beyond the length of the manufacturer's guarantee. Remember, if you are offered a three year extended warranty the first year may be duplicating what you already get for free (the manufacturer's guarantee). Your job is to weigh up the cost of the warranty against the replacement cost of the item you're buying. Questions to ask yourself:

- Will you be buying an upgrade or renewing the product within a few years anyway? If so, you probably won't benefit from a two or three year extended warranty.
- Will the item be used a lot? Are you the type of person who loses or damages things frequently? If you are, the extended warranty might be something to think about if you're planning to keep it for longer than a year.
- If you pay with a credit or debit card, does the card already insure your purchases? If in doubt, go to the card's web site or call the hotline to find out.
- If you have property insurance, does it cover such purchases?
- If you opt for the extended coverage, read the small print – does it cover loss, breakage, theft, or just malfunction?
- How reliable is the product? Read reviews and see if the product you are buying rarely breaks or malfunctions – if it does, you may not need more than the one-year guarantee the manufacturer gives you for free.

★ **Coupons and reward programs**. When making purchases at many stores, you will be asked if you want to sign up for the *reward program* or *membership program*. These programs will allow you to accumulate points and receive discounts on current and future purchases – definitely worth it if you're on a tight budget. You will also be given coupons, which you can use for future purchases at the same store.

★ **Self-checkout**. Many large stores now have self-checkout lanes, where you scan your items and pay without the help of a sales assistant. Although these checkouts often look quicker than the regular checkout lines, the machines are very sensitive and you often end up having to wait for assistance.

★ **Bag packers**. In supermarkets there is usually a second person at the checkout, who helps to pack your bags. If no one is there, by all means start packing your own bags, but if you insist on doing this when there is a packer to help, it often causes confusion. Americans don't tip the bag packer.

★ **Used goods**. There are lots of stores selling pre-owned or *used goods* in the USA. The quality varies, but these stores typically do a great job of weeding out worn or otherwise unsuitable items, and if you're on a budget it's a great place to find jeans for under $10 and so on. Such stores are called *thrift* stores, *rummage* stores, *goodwill* or *Salvation Army* stores among other names. A *consignment* store sells clothes on behalf of other customers – the quality is usually better and the prices slightly higher.

★ **Sales tax**. The number you see on the price tag isn't usually the amount you're required to pay. With few exceptions, states collect a sales tax on top of the price of an item – the sales tax percentage differs from state to state and is normally within the 1-10% range. When the sales assistant tells you the amount you owe, this figure will include the sales tax.

★ **Clothing sizes**. Although it's probably safer to try clothes on until you get used to the sizing and the fit, in general, American sizes convert as follows:
- US to European – for women's clothing, the US size number is generally two sizes below the UK equivalent, so if you're a size 12 in the UK, or a 40 in France, start with a size 8 in the US.
- Shoe sizes – women's shoe size numbers are bigger than the UK version. A size 9 in the US is a size 7 in the UK or a 40 European.

📖 FURTHER READING
For clothing and shoe conversions for many sizing charts, Size Guide is a great web reference with many examples and comparisons – www.sizeguide.net.

Telephone information

Every country is assigned an exit code for making phone calls outside the country, and an entry code for international calls coming into the country. The country (entry) code for the USA is 1, which must be used when calling the USA from overseas. The exit code when calling abroad from the USA (also known as the IDD – International Direct Dialing prefix) is 011:

★ International callers to the USA dial the international exit code from their country (usually 00) +1+ Area Code + 7-digit phone number. There are many web sites providing area codes in the USA and area codes are always three-digit numbers – www.allareacodes.com gives area codes by city and allows you to search for an area code in a number of different ways.

★ When dialing long distance within the USA, you will need the area code plus the 7-digit phone number of the person you're calling. Before dialing these numbers you must first dial 1. When dialing someone in the same location, many areas still have to dial 1 plus the area code, even if the area code is the same as yours, although in a few places you can simply dial the 7-digit phone number.

★ There is no difference between calling a landline or cell phone, as both have numbers with an area code plus 7-digits.

★ When giving out your own phone number you should always include the area code too, as some large cities have more than one area code.

★ When calling abroad from the USA you must use the US exit code – 011 – and then the relevant country code. There are many web sites that provide calling code information, for example – www.howtocallabroad.com is easy to use and gives country codes together with city area codes.

★ If the international number you are dialing from the USA begins with a 0 (zero), you usually have to drop the zero after dialing the country code.

Texting abbreviations

As most students seem to use their phones to text rather than talk, you'll need to know the American abbreviations:

ABT	–	about
AKA	–	also known as
ASAP	–	as soon as possible
ATM	–	at the moment
B4	–	before
BC	–	because
BFD	–	big friggin' deal
B/F	–	boyfriend
BFF	–	best friend forever
BTW	–	by the way
CM	–	call me
CU	–	see you
CUL8R	–	see you later
DKDC	–	don't know don't care
EVA	–	ever
F2F	–	face to face
FAQ	–	frequently asked questions
FB	–	Facebook
G2CU	–	great to see you
GF	–	girl friend
GNITE	–	good night
GR8	–	great
HRU	–	how are you?
HW	–	homework
IA8	–	I already ate
IDBI	–	I don't believe it

IDC	–	I don't care
IDK	–	I don't know
IDTS	–	I don't think so
IK	–	I know
IM	–	instant message
IMO	–	in my opinion
IMHO	–	in my humble opinion
K	–	okay
L8	–	late
LMAO	–	laughing my a** off
LMFAO	–	laughing my freaking a** off
LMK	–	let me know
LOL	–	laugh(ing) out loud
MIRL	–	meet in real life
MSG	–	message
NBD	–	no big deal
OMG	–	oh my god
OTFL	–	on the floor laughing
PLZ	–	please
POV	–	point of view
R	–	are
RBAY	–	right back at you
ROFL	–	rolling on the floor laughing
RSVP	–	please reply (actually, Repondez S'il Vous Plait)
RU	–	are you
SUP	–	what's up?
SYL	–	see you later
SYS	–	see you soon
TBC	–	to be continued
TBD	–	to be determined
TBH	–	to be honest
THX	–	thanks
TGIF	–	thank God it's Friday
TMI/2MI	–	too much information
TTYL	–	talk to you later

TTYS	–	talk to you soon
UR	–	your or you're
VM	–	voicemail
W@	–	what?
W8	–	wait
WDYK	–	what do you know?
WDYT	–	what do you think?
W/E	–	weekend
WK	–	week
WKD	–	weekend
WRU@	–	where are you at?
Y	–	why
ZZZ	–	sleeping, or bored
2G2BT	–	too good to be true
2MOR	–	tomorrow
2NTE	–	tonight
411	–	information
4U	–	for you
@	–	at

This isn't an exhaustive list and new acronyms appear all the time.

Town and city layouts

Many villages, towns and cities are laid out on the grid system. Looking at a map, roads and streets run north-south (vertically) and east-west (horizontally) almost exclusively. They will also have a block number allowing people to know exactly where they are in the town, and where they are in relation to other street addresses.

For example, in Chicago, the intersection of State and Madison is 0 (zero). A street address that is 2200 North Lincoln means it is 22 blocks north of the 0 (zero) position on the map – therefore it is 22 blocks north of Madison Avenue. A street that is 1100 west, is located 11 blocks west of State Street. Many streets have alphabet letters or numerals as their actual name, making it even easier to find your way around.

Take the time to learn how to use this grid system and it will make getting around much easier. The main thing you need to figure out is the location of north, south, east and west, as most Americans will use this when giving you directions. Find landmarks north, south, east and west of your dorm for example, and this will help avoid setting out in the wrong direction when you leave the building.

📖 **FURTHER READING**
The government's explanation of the US grid system – http://www.fgdc.gov/usng/how-to-read-usng/index_html.

Weather

As mentioned in *Chapter Three – What to Consider When Choosing a College*, the USA is a vast country and the weather can be markedly different depending on where you choose to study. There can also be dramatic extremes in the summer and winter in a particular region. For example, many areas in the mid-west have hot summers and extremely cold winters. If you are from a fairly warm or mild climate, think carefully about colleges in northern states with severe winters, as the winters are also long. In states like Minnesota you can spend five months in weather that is below freezing. This, in turn, requires a wardrobe of clothing you probably don't have.

Southern states, on the other hand, can be excessively hot in the summer, and the months either side of summer can be pretty warm too. There are also bugs such as ticks and mosquitoes that might make things more difficult for you.

If you attend college in a location with extreme temperatures, pay attention to the forecasts and advice given by locals and the experts. If the TV weather person tells you not to go out because of frostbite concerns, stay indoors. If there is a heat advisory, make sure to keep yourself hydrated and out of the sun.

Weights and measures

You may be surprised to learn that, for the most part, the USA has not switched over to the metric system. Measurements are in feet and inches, and weight is still measured in pounds and ounces. Oven temperatures are mostly in degrees Fahrenheit, as are national and local weather forecasts.

You'll find this conversion chart useful as it allows you to enter a number and get its conversion in metric or Imperial/ US customary – http://www.metric-conversions.org/. It comes in several different languages and has a very useful smart phone app:

★ One measurement you might not be familiar with is a *cup*. Many recipes call for ingredients in cup quantities and people often refer to this measurement when trying to give you an idea of quantity. A cup is a measurement of *volume* rather than weight, so recipes can call for a cup of sugar, a cup of lettuce or a cup of rice. The cup refers to an actual measuring tool and not any old cup you happen to find lying around. If you're into cooking, you should probably buy yourself a cheap plastic cup measure.

Emergency information

It is important to know how to call for help should you find yourself in dangerous or life-threatening situations:

★ Find out how to contact your college's own campus police department and use this number when an ambulance or fire engine is not needed. Campus police may be able to respond to your emergency faster than the town or county police.

★ 911 is the nationwide telephone number for emergency services in the USA. You can call for police officers, ambulances and fire, personnel using this number. Do not use this number for annoying, but non-emergency, situations or you could find yourself in trouble for wasting police or paramedic time:
  - If you call from a landline (i.e. not a cell phone), the operator answering your call will usually be able to tell where you are. If the emergency is not happening at the same location, tell the operator immediately and give the exact address.
  - If you are using a cell phone to make a 911 call, the operator will probably not know your location so this is the first piece of information you should give. Before placing the call, make sure you know exactly where you are or have someone with you who can tell you the street address.
  - Government guidelines advise you to give your cell phone number to the operator, who will be able to call you back if you are cut off – http://www.fcc.gov/guides/wireless-911-services
  - If you are calling for medical assistance stay on the line, as the operator will very often advise you until the paramedics arrive.
  - You should also consider entering ICE contact information into your cell phone. ICE stands for *In Case of Emergency* and allows people to find the numbers of individuals to contact in case something happens to you. If you have the numbers of family members outside of the USA, remember to input the entire telephone number a caller would need when calling from the USA.

★ Many areas in the USA have an alternate number for non-emergencies. Usually this number is 311 but you should not assume this covers your location.

Chapter Twelve
Notes For Parents

Although it's important your high schooler takes charge of his or her college application, I would strongly advise you to skim, if not read, this book to get an idea of what the process entails.

Rena Nathanson, the mother of a British/ American son applying to US colleges, advises parents to get involved and support the student in the application process, which she describes as, "very stressful" and at times, "a struggle". She also warns parents about the brutality of the system, "Your child is not special. You may think s/ he is but in the application system s/ he's just a number."

Your teen will want your input and there are some things you may want to consider as you guide/ support him/ her through the process of making a college choice:

★ It is generally recognized that students perform better if they are studying at a college they actually want to attend, but your teenager may still want your opinion on the various US college options, and as you're likely to be footing the bill in full or in part, you'll probably want some say. There are various web sites giving lists and rankings of US colleges and universities using a number of

different criteria. A few are listed here and there are many more in the resources section at the end of the book:
- The Fiske Guide to Colleges – http://www.fiskeguide.com
- Kiplinger '*best value guide*' – http://www.kiplinger.com
- Princeton Review – http://www.princetonreview.com
- Best colleges – http://www.thebestcolleges.org

★ There are thousands of colleges in the USA, and you may not have heard of many of them. Because you don't recognize the college your student is talking about doesn't mean it's not a good college. Some of the smallest and least internationally known colleges rank very highly in the USA. Similarly, if your student is only focusing on the 'big name' US colleges, encourage him or her to look further afield. Some colleges excel in very specific academic fields, yet may not rank among the top *overall* colleges. If your student has an interest in Engineering, Journalism or Business for example, use the web sites above to find the best colleges in those fields.

★ Before your student starts at his or her college, you will probably receive something in the mail – a request for donations, thinly disguised as a welcome letter. American colleges have never been wholly state-funded and most have never received regular government funding, relying heavily on donations from current and past parents, and former students. Fund-raising is big business and there are whole departments given over to persuading people to donate money. Obviously they don't call themselves donation-chasers or even fund-raisers. The term used by many organizations trying to raise money is *Development* and it's very often tied in with *Alumni Relations* or *Student Affairs*.

Visit almost any American college web site and there will be a tab for 'Parents'. Your involvement in your child's US academic life doesn't end when you put them on the plane.

Parental involvement

So prevalent are *Parent Programs* in American college life that the University of Minnesota regularly conducts the *National Survey of College and University Parent Programs* – http://www1.umn.edu/parent/about/survey-reports/index.html. This gives a great snapshot of common practices and general trends. There is even an Association of Higher Education Parent/ Family Program Professionals and an accompanying web site – http://www.aheppp.org/.

Also look at the College parents of America web site – http://www.collegeparents.org founded: '*to assist families in the successful preparation, transition, adjustment and completion through college*'. Member benefits include advice on obtaining tuition refunds in cases of withdrawals for medical reasons, tax advice, insurance plans and discounted admissions counseling:

★ As a parent you can become very involved with your child's college, as private institutions frequently have parent trustees on the Board. Colleges have various organizations for parents, such as Boston University's *Parent Program*, designed: '*to keep parents engaged and informed*'. Duke University has a *Parents Advisory Council* with one of its objectives being: '*to provide an outlet for parents of students who want to be involved in the undergraduate Duke Experience*'. Many colleges have a parent program at orientation, whereby your student goes off to his/ her own orientation, and the parents go elsewhere to hear about what the student will be learning. Attendance is rarely mandatory.

★ Most of your communication with the college will be in the form of regular e-mails, telling you everything from on-campus security to upcoming speakers, and what the Dean is doing. If representatives of the college are visiting near to you, perhaps on a recruitment drive, don't be surprised to receive a phone call inviting you to a breakfast or evening event. A few colleges don't e-mail parents on a regular basis, but I can't promise this.

★ The upside to this communication from the college is that it can work both ways. If you think there's a problem your college student isn't telling you about, or perhaps isn't coping with, the appropriate advisors at his/ her college can often intervene in a way that is acceptable to both student and parent. E-mail the 'Parent' e-mail address on the web site, and you'll be directed to the appropriate individual. More importantly, if they think you are behaving like a *helicopter parent*, they will probably advise you to allow the student to handle it in his/ her own time.

 WARNING
A helicopter parent is one who is too involved in their child's (usually) academic life and does not let their child take care of his or her own affairs.

A word about *helicopter parents*. While it seems to be on the wane slightly, extreme helicopter parenting has been a problem for many US colleges. Examples (which might be urban myths) include parents who insist on daughters being in dorm rooms by 8 pm and calling campus security to enforce this, a father complaining his daughter had been offered milk when she was lactose intolerant, and a mother who scheduled every minute of her son's day, complete with spreadsheets. (Examples courtesy of *College Confidential*.) There is even a company offering audio conference tapes for college professionals entitled, *Difficult Parents on Campus; Tips to Handle 'Helicopter' Behavior* – https://www.pbconferences.com/audio/main.asp?G=2&E=1048&I=1. If the word 'helicopter' is used by anyone from your child's college, take the hint you might be interfering too much.

★ **Parents' Weekend**. One tradition you might not be familiar with is Parents' Weekend. It usually occurs about a month after students have started classes in the fall/ autumn and is a weekend at the college crammed with activities for parents and siblings. Many parents attend although, not surprisingly, overseas parents often don't and aren't expected to. I would recommend attending at least the freshman weekend if you can, as it's a great way to meet your student's friends and generally get an idea of what college life will be like for him or her.

> ⚠ **WARNING**
> If you plan to visit your son/ daughter's college at a time when many families will also be visiting, make your hotel reservations well in advance. Not only do rooms book up quickly, you'll probably find the prices get higher as the weekend approaches. Your college web site will usually have links to nearby hotels.

★ **Care packages**. Care packages are a big thing in the USA, and students are frequently sent parcels of varying sizes stuffed full of goodies. If the cost of mailing something from your country to the USA is not worthwhile, there are many delivery options, including web sites specializing in care packages. Examples include – www.carepackages.com, www.hipkits.com and www.from-mom.com. Particularly around exam time, you may receive a mailing or an e-mail from your child's college reminding you to send a care package and pointing out that if you don't, your child may be the only one in his/ her group of friends not to receive something in the mail!

★ **FERPA**. Federal Educational Rights and Privacy Act. Although FERPA was passed to protect student records and information, it may surprise parents to learn that although they are funding their child's tuition and expenses, they are denied access to educational information unless their child consents to disclosure. *Educational information* includes grades, disciplinary records, class schedules, personal information and enrolment records. In other words, if your child doesn't want to tell you what classes s/ he's taking or how s/ he is doing, you can't go to the college to find out. However, many colleges do have a waiver/ consent form students can sign and have put on their file, allowing parents to be given certain information about the student.

There are a few exceptions to this rule and the US government states that FERPA permit a school to disclose personally identifiable information from education records of an *eligible student* (i.e. a student age 18 or older or enrolled in a postsecondary institution at any age) to his or her parents if the student is a *dependent student* as defined in Section 152 of the Internal Revenue Code: '*Generally, if either parent has claimed the student as a dependent on the parent's most recent income tax statement, the school may non-consensually disclose the student's education records to both parents under this exception.*'

Personally identifiable information may also be disclosed to parents (and other relevant third parties), without consent, in connection with a health and safety emergency, or where the student has violated federal, state or local laws, or the college's regulations, regarding the use of possession of alcohol or a controlled substance. Your student's college may have its own policy with regard to alcohol-related incidents and what parents are told.

📖 FURTHER READING
The government web site gives full details of FERPA here – http://www2.ed.gov/policy/gen/guid/fpco/ferpa/students.html

Depending on the college, FERPA rules may also mean you are not included in disciplinary procedures brought against your student. Many colleges want college students to deal with problems themselves, and may actively discourage, if not prevent, you from getting involved. While writing this book I was told of a student who was hospitalized because of excess alcohol use. It was the college's policy not to inform parents, but the parents in question happened to be in town on the same night and were outraged at not having been notified. If you're a parent who feels strongly about being informed of certain situations your student may find him or herself in, make sure you understand the college's policies on this.

Student support

Your student may be thousands of miles away from you during term time, and it's natural for parents to worry. At American colleges there are an impressive number of professionals available to guide and support your son or daughter:

★ **Advisors**. In most cases there will be an academic advisor, a professor and a TA (Teaching Assistant) to help with academic matters, an RA (Resident Assistant), Dorm Proctor and Housing specialists to help with housing matters, mental health professionals on campus, learning specialists and free tutors, as well as a medical facility. There is also an International Students Office and a DSO (Designated School Official) for all matters relating to the Non-Immigrant status. Encourage your student to go to any one of these professionals for help as soon as it is needed.

★ **Mental health professionals**. Colleges have mental health professionals on hand day and night to give support and counseling to students. There will be signs posted around the campus with phone numbers to call, and a dedicated page on the web site. In the USA there is **no** stigma in seeking out emotional guidance and it is always confidential – students are encouraged to ask for help before a problem or concern becomes too much for them to handle.

★ **Dropping out**. It is not uncommon for American students to drop out and transfer to a different college after a semester or a year. Whatever their reasons for wanting out, it is generally not seen as failure, but a chance to get back on the right track. If they transfer to a new college, international students must obtain a new I-20 from this college to maintain their visa status.

Financial matters

Tuition deposit and payment

When your son or daughter accepts a college offer, this acceptance must be accompanied by a tuition deposit or *enrollment confirmation* payment. This amount is typically $500 – $1,000 and is non-refundable, although it will be applied to subsequent tuition payments. Telling the Admissions office your student is definitely accepting the offer will not usually start the ball rolling – official paperwork accepting the offer **must** be submitted:

★ Although your student will have to show ability to pay for a year at college when applying for the student visa, this payment doesn't have to be made all at one time. Most colleges bill by the semester and many offer the option to pay in installments throughout the academic year. Details will be found on the web site, and Admissions staff members can help too.

Hidden costs

As you will have gathered, studying in the USA can be expensive. What many people don't appreciate before submitting applications are the hidden costs in the process. Please refer to *Chapter One –*

Thinking of Studying in the USA? for a list of these extra fees and costs. (See *Chapter Five – The College Application Process*, and *Chapter Seven – Offers and Rejections*, for specifics on application and visa costs.)

Budgeting

Before your student leaves for college establish and discuss the amount of money you can provide as an allowance, and how it should be managed:

★ For many teens, having a relatively large sum of money at their disposal is a new experience. Reactions will range from blowing it all in the first two weeks, to being so afraid of running out of money they exist on bread for the entire semester. If your student has never had to manage his/ her own money before, I advise having a discussion about weekly budgeting. As parents, you should also have a plan as to how you will respond should your student go over budget, and your student should be aware of these consequences.

★ If your child is planning to find employment on arrival at campus, this should be factored into the money they have to spend, but remember the job may not materialize for a few weeks.

★ It is difficult to suggest a suitable weekly allowance for your student as the cost of living varies widely throughout the USA. If possible, have your student ask on the student forums what the average weekly spending amount is. Although s/ he will receive a variety of answers, it may be possible to get an average amount from the information.

Banking

Banking options are covered in *Chapter Eight – Before You Go – Visa Application and Other Important Steps*. It is fairly simple to open an American checking (current or non-savings) account once the student has arrived in the USA. This will probably mean your money has to be transferred from your bank to the American account, and you should first check with your own bank how this can be done. Before your student opens an account, have him/ her find out from that bank, what forms of money transfer they can accept. The International Students Office on campus will often be able to give advice to students too.

For details on financial aid in the form of scholarships, grants, and loans, please refer to *Chapter Four – Funding your College Degree*.

Insurance

There are various types of insurance you should think about:

★ **Health insurance**. Details about Health Insurance are covered in *Chapter Eight – Before You Go – Visa Application and Other Important Steps*, but I must stress this is a very important issue. Most colleges will insist on proof that your student is covered by health/ medical insurance, whether it is purchased in your own country or from the college's partner providers. It is worth reading about the coverage offered by the college as it is often very reasonably priced. Whatever your coverage, make sure your student finds out what is covered **before** receiving medical care. If they are attending a language proficiency class or any other class before the semester officially starts, the health insurance may not cover this period.

If you think insurance premiums are expensive, a quick look at medical costs in the USA will convince you the coverage is worth it. A simple visit to a doctor usually costs at least $100, and further treatment is alarmingly expensive. An article in the *Washington Post* (Mar 2, 2012) reported the average cost of a CT scan in the USA was over $500, an MRI would cost approximately $1,000 while an appendectomy costs around $13,000. Each day spent in a hospital runs up a bill of almost $4,000. Although your insurance company would contribute toward these costs, in most cases there will be a balance to pay that could run into thousands of dollars.

If your student visits the campus student clinic, the cost for those services is often deducted from their student account and the paperwork is then submitted to the health insurance company for reimbursement. Make sure your student understands the procedure and keeps all paperwork relating to healthcare.

★ **Property insurance**. Your student's college will also offer property insurance for items s/ he will have in the dorm room. This is not usually mandatory so you should compare the annual cost of premiums versus the cost of replacing whatever is damaged or stolen. To prevent theft, you can buy safes that fit under standard dorm beds, and there are cables to prevent computer theft.

★ **Tuition reimbursement insurance**. As foreign students have to prove ability to pay for the first year of tuition as part of visa eligibility, parents are usually heavily involved in the finances. You might wonder what happens to the fees you have paid, should your college student have to withdraw before the end of the semester. Many colleges offer some form of tuition reimbursement on a sliding scale – the longer your son or daughter is at the college, the smaller the refund. The cut off for any refund is often only a few weeks into the semester, after which there is no refund at all. For this reason, there are now a handful of companies offering a tuition refund plan to complement individual college refund policies:
- Individual college web sites will have information on their tuition refund policies, including exceptions and exclusions. Third party tuition refund plans usually make up the difference in the refund from the college. For example, if the college offers 50%, the plan will cover the remaining 50%.
- Most coverage is for physical and mental health withdrawals only, and requires an official withdrawal as well as written

statements from a doctor. As most young adults are fairly robust individuals, many parents take the risk they will be able to complete the semester. If your student hasn't always been in 100% health, it might be something worth considering. Unfortunately many policies exclude pre-existing conditions, or conditions present in the previous six or twelve months.

- The following companies offer tuition refund plans:
  ▷ AWG Dewars Inc. – www.collegerefund.com
  ▷ Education Insurance Plans (EIP) – http://educationinsuranceplans.com
  ▷ Markel Insurance – http://www.markelinsurance.com/Products/AandH/Pages/TuitionRefund.aspx
  ▷ GradGuard Tuition Insurance is a group policy with College Parents of America – www.gradguard.com/tuition

Taxes

The US Government's IRS (Internal Revenue Service) requires all international students and their dependents to file a US Federal Tax return each year. Filing a tax return does not necessarily mean you or your student owe any money in taxes. This is explained in *Chapter Ten – US College Life – The Lowdown*, and links to the relevant government web pages are provided.

It goes without saying that college life today is completely different from a generation ago, mainly because of technology. Everything from buying textbooks to submitting homework assignments is done online, so don't be surprised to find yourself saying, "In my day…" Furthermore, American college life is very different from its foreign cousins, and you may find, before long, your college child is speaking a completely different language!

As a soon-to-be college parent you may find the following web sites useful:

★ **Video College Advisor** – http://www.facebook.com/b4collegevideos – a Facebook page with videos from seasoned college admissions professionals and student coaches

★ **Parents countdown to college coach** – http://www.parentscountdowntocollegecoach.com/

★ **College Tips for Parents** – www.collegetipsforparents.org

★ **College Mom Minute** – http://www.smartcollegevisit.com/college-mom-minute/

★ **College Parents** – www.collegeparents.org

★ **Parents and Colleges** – http://www.parentsandcolleges.com

★ **The Neurotic Parent** – http://neuroticparent.typepad.com/

Resources

Web sites

Please note – all web sites cited in this book, with particular reference to government web sites, are prone to changes in design and format which may affect their URLs.

Government and official

https://ceac.state.gov/genniv/
US Department of State DS-160 Non-Immigrant Visa Application guidelines and forms

http://www.chea.org/
Council for Higher Education Accreditation

www.cbp.gov
The official US Customs and Border Protection web site

http://www.educationusa.state.gov/
The Department of State's official guide to studying in the USA. Helping foreign students narrow down the choice of colleges

https://www.fmjfee.com/i901fee/index.jsp
SEVP web site to pay and track I-901 SEVIS fees

http://www.ice.gov/sevis/
ICE (Immigration and Customs Enforcement) with detailed
information on SEVIS and step-by-step instructions on applications

http://www.irs.gov/Individuals/International-Taxpayers/Foreign-Students-and-Scholars
The Internal Revenue Services page for foreign students

http://studyinthestates.dhs.gov
The Government's *Study in the States* web site, giving overviews,
comprehensive information and links to other web pages. An
'*innovative information hub for the International student community*'

http://travel.state.gov
US Department of State web site giving a great overview and FAQs
about foreign student visas. Also has information on visa wait
times at embassies throughout the world

www.schengenvisa.cc
Information about required transit visas

www.usacollegeday.eventbrite.co.uk
Fulbright's information on US college fairs

http://ope.ed.gov/accreditation
The US government's list of accredited colleges

http://www.uscis.gov/portal/site/uscis
US Citizenship and Immigration Services giving a basic
explanation of types of student visas

http://www.usembassy.gov/
US Department of State, listing US embassies and consulates around the world

General college information (does not include consulting web sites)

http://www.collegedata.com
A comprehensive web site to guide students through college, application, and financial aid searches

http://www.collegexpress.com
Free registration for online college and scholarship searching. In return for the free service, individuals may be contacted by colleges and marketing professions

www.collegeconfidential.com
'*The world's largest college forum*' covering an array of topics and a free member forum

www.collegeview.com
Hobson's web site for students and parents seeking college-related information

www.collegeweeklive.com
Free online college fairs

http://www.edupass.org
Provides information to international students thinking about studying in the USA

www.iau-aiu.net
International Association of Universities

http://international.collegeboard.org
A resource to help students from around the world attain first/
undergraduate degrees at top-rated universities and specialized
institutions

www.nacacnet.org
The National Association for College Admissions Counselors

http://www.nafsa.org
The web site of the Association of International Educators

http://www.petersons.com
'*Everything you need to know about getting into the school you want*'

www.thebestcolleges.org
Princeton Review's guide to colleges

http://www.thecollegesolution.com/
A comprehensive blog by a veteran in the business

www.topuniversities.com
Country guides, university rankings and course information for
undergraduate students

http://www.uniintheusa.com/
A British guide to universities in the USA and beyond

www.usaeducationguides.com
A resource for international students hoping to study in the USA

http://wise.wisefoundation.com
The Worldwide International Student Exchange program

Academic information

www.aacc.nche.edu
The American Association of Community Colleges

www.act.org and www.actstudent.org
The official web sites for the ACT standardized college entrance exams

www.collegedata.com
A web site allowing students to calculate their college admission chances

www.commonapp.org
The official web site for the Common Application, widely used by US college Admissions offices

www.fairtest.org/university/optional
The National Center for Fair and Open Testing with list of test optional colleges

http://foreign.fulbrightonline.org
The US government's Fulbright Program for foreign students wishing to study in the USA

www.ibo.org
Information on the International Baccalaureate®

www.ielts.org
An English Language Proficiency testing company

www.kaptest.com
An established ACT/ SAT test prep company

www.naces.org
The National Association of Credential Evaluation Services. Some colleges will ask foreign applicants to use these companies

www.pearsonpte.com
An English Language Proficiency testing company

www.plagiarism.org
Information about plagiarism, and a means to test documents for plagiarism

www.ratemyprofessors.com
A student-written web site with ratings of individual professors and specific colleges

www.toeflgoanywhere.org
An English Language Proficiency testing company

http://turnitin.com
Examines documents for plagiarism

www.universalcollegeapp.com
The official web site for the Universal College application, used by a relatively small number of colleges

College search

Many of the general web sites include college search options, but the following are more targeted:

www.bigfuture.collegeboard.org/college-search
A comprehensive college search tool from the College Board

www.cappex.com
A free web site where students can create a profile and find college matches

http://colleges.collegetoolkit.com/CommunityToolkit/CanIGetIn/
Search/BySATACT.aspx
Allows you to search for colleges using your ACT or SAT scores as
a match

www.collegeconfidential.com
A free forum for asking any questions about American colleges

www.collegedata.com
Allows students to search for the right college fit using multiple criteria

www.collegeprowler.com
A college information and search web site written by students,
for students

www.collegeview.com
Hobson's web site giving lots of information on US colleges and a
search tool for applicants to find the right college

www.educationusa.info
Details of international college fairs in various regions around the world

www.hobsonsevents.com –
Hobson's virtual college fairs

www.iie.org
Institute of International Education

www.internationalstudent.com
A portal for students wishing to study overseas with country
specific information

www.petersons.com/college-search
Peterson's college search web site allowing students to search by
various criteria

www.princetonreview.com
The *Princeton Review's* web site – a test prep and college guidance organization

http://universityfairs.com
College fairs around the world

www.usacollegeday.eventbrite.co.uk
The Fulbright Commission's free college fairs in London

Finance and scholarship

http://bigfuture.collegeboard.org/scholarship-search
The College Board's web site with a college search

www.campusexplorer.com
Campus Explorer allows you to search for scholarships by major, by state or by college.

http://collegecost.ed.gov
The US Department of Education's *College Affordability and Transparency Center*, providing information on tuition and net prices

http://collegestats.org/colleges/all/lowest-outofstate-cost
Lists of the lowest tuition rates for out-of-state students

www.collegeweeklive.com
CollegeWeekLive is a 'free online event' designed to help prospective students. It has regularly updated information on available scholarships

http://www.collegerefund.com/
Dewar's tuition refund web site

www.college-scholarships.com
A list of over 50 free online scholarship search sites

http://www.edupass.org/finaid/undergraduate.phtml
A list of colleges awarding scholarships to international students.
(Does not include colleges giving few financial awards or those
awarding sports scholarships to international students.)

www.fastweb.com
A free resource covering how to pay for college, including scholarships

http://www.finaid.org/
'*the smart student guide to financial aid*'

http://fulbright.state.gov
Information on financial aid specific to your country or region

http://www.ibo.org/diploma/recognition/scholarships/
International Baccalaureate lists worldwide scholarships available
for holders of the IB

http://www.iefa.org/
International financial aid and college scholarship search

http://www.iie.org/en/What-We-Do/Fellowship-And-Scholarship-
Management
Institute of International Education (IIE) has a comprehensive list
of financial assistance available to foreign students coming to the
USA to study

www.internationalscholarships.com
Financial aid information and search capability for international
students

www.internationalstudentloan.com
International Student Loan – part of the International Student Network – Colleges must be listed as eligible

http://www.irs.gov/Individuals/International-Taxpayers/Foreign-Students-and-Scholars
The US government's web site covering foreign student tax issues

http://www.isoa.org/list_scholarships.aspx
The International Students Office (ISO) has a list of scholarships and grants on its web site

http://kiplinger.com/tools/colleges
Kiplinger's best value in public colleges list

www.porceline.net/freeapps/about.html
An updated list of colleges who don't charge for applications

http://profileonline.collegeboard.com
The CSS profile, which many colleges require. Information and instructions on how to complete the form

www.questbridge.org
'Connecting the world's brightest low-income students to America's best universities and opportunities'. Includes a limited number of financial aid possibilities for non-US citizens

http://www.scholars4dev.com/6499/scholarships-in-usa-for-international-students/
Links to many US colleges offering financial aid to international students from developing countries

http://studentaid.ed.gov/eligibility/non-us-citizens
A guide to US Federal Aid programs, including information on eligibility

http://www.studentloannetwork.com
A web site explaining student loan options, with a forum and search mechanism

www.ussapglobal.org
United States Achievers Program – programs in sixteen countries on four continents offering resources to obtain scholarships

Athletic related

www.berecruited.com
An '*online networking destination for high school student-athletes seeking recruitment from college coaches and universities*'

www.college-athletic-scholarships.com
American Educational Guidance Center's web site with comprehensive information on athletic scholarships

http://www.collegerecruitingwebsite.com
A fee based service allowing potential student athletes to build a profile and be seen by college coaches

www.collegescholarhips.org/athletic.htm
'*Helping students pay for college since 1999*'

http://www.ncaapublications.com/productdownloads/IS10.pdf
The NCAA's Guide to International Academic Standards for Athletics eligibility

http://recruiting-101.com
Information for Athletes, parents and coaches

For parents

http://www.parentscountdowntocollegecoach.com/
Parents countdown to college coach

www.collegetipsforparents.org
College tips for parents

http://www.smartcollegevisit.com/college-mom-minute/
College Mom Minute

www.collegeparents.org
College parents

Books and articles

Paying for College Without Going Broke, Kalman A. Chany,
The Princeton Review, Random House Inc., New York, 2012

The Global Nomad's Guide to University Transition, Tina L. Quick,
Summertime Publishing, 2010

10 Colleges that Give the Most International Student Financial Aid,
Katy Hopkins, US News, October 16, 2012

Also Published by summertimepublishing

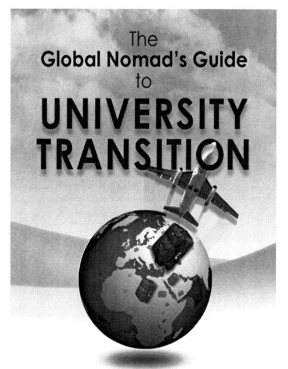

The
Global Nomad's Guide
to
UNIVERSITY
TRANSITION

Tina L. Quick

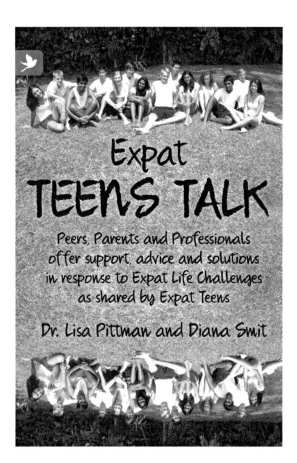

Expat
TEENS TALK

Peers, Parents and Professionals
offer support, advice and solutions
in response to Expat Life Challenges
as shared by Expat Teens

Dr. Lisa Pittman and Diana Smit

THE EMOTIONALLY RESILIENT EXPAT

Engage, Adapt and Thrive Across Cultures

"Groundbreaking..."
Ruth E. Van Reken
Author of *Third Culture Kids*

LINDA A. JANSSEN